THE RIDE

A True Story of Finding Freedom Behind Bars

LARRY ANDREWS

Michael,

I hope you enjoy The Ride!

Praise for *The Ride*

"Larry has an amazing testimony of the grace of God. I've heard dozens of stories about jailhouse conversions and second chances, but Larry has made the most of his opportunities. His conversion hasn't been simply an emotional response to getting caught, but a consistent life change. The "new" Larry Andrews has impacted not only his family, but hundreds of people around him and anyone he meets or comes in contact with. This story will challenge you to make the most of your "second chances" and hopefully help you see a God who has a plan for us that is much bigger than our wildest dreams."

Rob McClure, Assistant Pastor, The Bridge – Mustang, OK

"An intriguing true story of redemption, hope, and new beginnings. *The Ride* will be a breath of fresh air to those trapped by the consequences of bad choices and haunted by dying dreams. Parents and families will find renewed hope that the one you love can be made whole and return home. I have seen up close the new creation and the continued transformation of Larry Andrews. Expect to be impacted by a story that points to a Savior who can change the heart and destiny of a man."

Dr. Kenneth Isom, Associate Pastor,
The Bridge – Mustang, OK; Chairman/President of the
Board, Adult and Teen Challenge of Oklahoma – Oklahoma
City, OK; and Doctor of Veterinary Medicine Emeritus

"I know you will be blessed as you read the thrilling testimony of the love and mercy of the Lord in the life of Larry Andrews. You will see that the arm of the Lord is never too short to reach you, no matter how far away, or how deep in sin you may be. It is indeed a miracle to see how the Lord is using him to influence the lives of others. He is a great blessing to us here in Mustang, so just join us in *The Ride*."

Kenneth McGee, Associate Pastor,
The Bridge – Mustang, OK

"Larry Andrews' life is a monument to God's Grace! My first meeting with Larry was in a prison where he was looking at a lengthy sentence. As a pastor, I was visiting him at the request of someone in his family. I had no idea how great a blessing was in store for me as we began our friendship and fellowship. To see our Lord move Larry's heart and life from what the world sees as success to the despair of prison looked like defeat. But it was here that that magnificent, still small voice could be heard – and it was heard loud and clear. Like Paul, Larry was set free in prison and eventually from prison by the grace of God. It was here that Christ made Larry a new man – no less driven, but now driven in a new and wonderful direction. Now Larry found the joy of exalting his new-found Savior, and that has been and continues to be his mission and goal as God has blessed his marriage, his business, his music, and his witness. Larry's testimony continues to be a challenge and encouragement to anyone who will hear it, and the extent of its impact will only be realized when we get to glory!"

Fred Greening, Director of Employee Development and
Corporate Chaplain, B&H Construction – Goldsby, OK; and
retired pastor, Goldsby Baptist Church – Goldsby, OK

"Larry Andrews' story testifies to one of the most powerful words in our language. It is the word HOPE. Staring at the reality of spending the prime of his life in a prison cell, God's grace reached him just when he needed it most. The redemption Larry received is a signal and encouragement that ALL men and women can experience the loving transformation of Jesus Christ! No one is outside of His reach, and if we humbly come to God, He will receive us and truly do loving and unexplainable miracles in our lives. I challenge you to simply read Larry's story. It is honest and straight-forward. He captures the shame of his failures and the glory of forgiven new life. I believe this book could help change your life!

Paul McGrady, Associate Athletic Director, Southern
Nazarene University – Bethany, OK

"Might you find yourself in an impossible situation with no escape? Read *The Ride* to find out how you got there and how to get out. You may have no other way or time."

Michael L. Galiga, Esq., Author of "Win
Every Battle" – Oklahoma City, OK

"I have known Larry Andrews for most of his life, as a business associate and family friend. I have seen the life he lived before Christ transformed him into the incredible man he has become. His new book, *The Ride,* outlines the miracles that had to happen to bring about his conversion; things that didn't happen by accident. I am honored to call him a friend. Every reader will be blessed by the true account of his real-life journey."

Gerald Grimes, Retired Former State Insurance Commissioner
of Oklahoma – Oklahoma City, Oklahoma

"*The Ride* puts you on the prison bus in a journey through the house of shame into a hope of God's making. Larry Andrews is faithful to tell his/God's story in this book that you will not be able to put down. It is a ride for those seeking to find victory in life. Larry found grace. I highly recommend this book for you and for your friends who seek the ride out of destructive lifestyles."

Dr. C. Wayne Childers, Retired Pastor – Oklahoma City, OK

"I came to know Larry Andrews when he brought my husband and me some fresh Colorado peaches and pears. What a wonderful time it was afterwards when, in return, he and his beautiful wife and precious children came over to our house for peach cobbler. When Larry told me his life's story that day, it didn't fit into the scenario there before me in my dining room. Surely, this man, who regularly attends our church, gifts an older couple with peaches and pears, works in the prison ministry, loves his wife and family, and has a thriving business, is exaggerating about his years in drugs, crime, and prison. But in his book, *The Ride*, Larry shows how "faith comes by hearing the Word of God." Larry Andrews is an example of one of those people who heard the Word of God, whose heart was touched by God, and his life was miraculously changed. Oh, that all of us can share the Word of God which is "light" to those who walk in darkness, a "path" to those who are lost, and "bread" and "living water" to those who hunger and thirst after righteousness."

Dr. Kathleen Wilcoxson, Former Oklahoma State
Senator and Bible Teacher – Oklahoma City, OK

"Larry Andrews was a student of mine in the late 1970's at Washington High School. He was a likable young man, a popular student, a good athlete, and from a fine, hardworking family. I thought he had a lot of potential. He and I talked about his plans for college, and I think he had aspirations for great things. After he graduated, he went on to college to play football and did well until he was injured. I didn't keep up with him much after that, but I did hear that he started a business and was doing very well. Sometimes success is a dangerous thing, and for him it was. As he will explain in *The Ride*, things went south for him. He sank to the point of spending time in prison. I didn't see his recovery, but I know it was a God thing. Years later, when I saw him in church, I could see that he had found a new mission in life. Today he serves God, and God has blessed him greatly."

Lynden Wilcoxson, Retired High School
Counselor and Teacher – Oklahoma City, OK

"I've only known Larry for less than a year, but I consider Larry to be a close friend. As a fellow builder and business man, and as a minister of the gospel, I recognize Larry's zeal for the gospel and that his relationship with God is very important to him. I had the privilege of visiting with the prosecuting attorney that was responsible for putting Larry in prison. He described Larry as a continual trouble maker for law enforcement before going to prison, and the remarkable change in Larry's life after finding Jesus as his savior. It is nothing less than a miracle. You won't forget this story of God's saving grace as you read this book. It will inspire you and give you faith for the salvation of your lost relatives and friends. I highly recommend *The Ride* as a great reading."

Rev. Wayne Long, Retired Pastor and Home
Builder – Oklahoma City, OK

"My ten-year journey with Larry Andrews is as a friend and fellow servant of Jesus Christ. I met this man after the toughest part of *The Ride* Today I know the new Larry…. the man whose life has been touched by the life changing power of Jesus Christ. I am the grateful recipient of friendship with a man whose life is rich in joy, peace, and an unashamed love for Jesus. Occasionally, we gather with friends who helped Larry through his darkest hour. We have coffee, we laugh, we talk about life, and especially enjoy hearing of God's grace as Larry takes us through the ups and downs of *The Ride*. Larry has a warm spirit, lots of funny stories, many sad stories, and above all, redemption stories about healing for himself and his family. *The Ride* is about God's miraculous grace. This book can be life altering for anyone at any age in any circumstance. It's uplifting. It's full of hope. It's a good read. I suggest that you read it, be encouraged by it, and then give it to someone who needs a blessing!"

Joe Grizzle, Retired Pastor, CrossPointe Church – Norman, OK

"I first met Larry Andrews years ago, when he introduced himself and then promptly asked me to accompany him to a home where young men were seeking help for drug and alcohol addiction. It was there, as I witnessed him share his heart, it became evident that Larry truly has a passion to help the hurting. In *The Ride*, Larry details his own story of how drug addiction took him to a very dark place and eventually to what some refer to as "hitting rock bottom". *The Ride* is not a story about recovery from addiction, but rather that complete freedom in Christ is available to anyone regardless of their current situation. Whether you are seeking help for yourself or someone you know, or just want to be inspired with a story about the grace, love, and long-suffering of our Lord, I recommend you read *The Ride*."

Wayne Gray, President and CEO, Adult and Teen
Challenge of Oklahoma – Oklahoma City, OK

"What an amazing book! *The Ride* will not only transform your deep appreciation for Larry Andrews' own personal journey, it will release God's healing and goodness into so many areas of your life! There's nothing more powerful than reading, declaring, and living out what God can do for those who create a personal relationship with our Master, **JESUS CHRIST**. Larry's mistakes, trials, and consequences will release faith, hope, and love into every walk of life for those who read it. As a successful home builder and roofing contractor, Larry must have many tools in his box to complete a project. *The Ride* leaves no tools missing in giving explicit examples and directions in following **JESUS**, while walking through daily dilemmas while living on earth."

Bill Farley, Director of Development, Oklahoma Jail and Prison
Ministries – Oklahoma City, OK; Former Athletic Director, University
of Central Oklahoma – Edmond, OK; Former Associate Athletic
Director, University of Alabama and University of Oklahoma

"I have known and prayed for Larry since the 1980's. During this time, I witnessed a period of self-destruction and decay to his life, which only a loving God could mend. On more than one such occasion, Larry informed me, with defiance, he was set on continuing his destructive ways. Even so, God never gave up on Larry. God's grace and mercy proved to be larger than all of Larry's detriment and pain. I am confident your life will be impacted as you read this powerful, life changing story of God's forgiveness, of second chance opportunities and how God chose to love Larry and set his feet on a new path."

Gerald Elrod, MBA, longtime friend and business associate – Oklahoma City, OK

"Larry's testimony will no doubt have a positive impact on people who are in need of encouragement, or a powerful message of God's grace and mercy. Thank you, Larry, for having the courage to share this amazing miracle of God's work in your life, and for reminding us that God's miracles are available to all of us!"

John Howry, Director, South OKC Area Youth for Christ – Oklahoma City, OK

"Larry Andrews and his life are clear examples of God's goodness and mercy following us throughout our lives. I have personally known Larry for close to 20 years and have experienced the same grace that he speaks of in his incredible story of hope and healing outlined in the pages you will read. Larry and I met behind prison walls as co-inmates, and I can remember speaking of a day like this when he would be able to tell his story (God's story) to the world. I am excited to see this amazing project, *The Ride*, come to life!"

Jed Chappell, Founder and CEO, City Center – Oklahoma City, OK

"I have known Larry Andrews my entire life, and have witnessed firsthand the mercy and grace God has given him. Growing up together, I always admired his drive and leadership qualities. I watched Larry's addiction use those qualities to take him down. But, I also saw Larry surrender his life to the Lord, and he became a gracious and kind man. He began using his gift of music and his testimony to minister to the broken. Larry is truly a changed man, and I am so proud of what God has done in his life. Larry is now one of my spiritual mentors, and he has been a strong influence in my personal recovery and walk with the Lord. *The Ride* will be a blessing to you as it has been to everyone who reads it. If God can change Larry's heart, God can change your heart! You only need to open your heart and mind to the Word of God, and let Him perform miracles in you as He did in Larry."

Doug Hayes, Facility Director, Rob's Ranch
Addiction Treatment Center – Purcell, OK

"Larry could not have come up with a better title, *The Ride*. I met Larry on his journey at my former job in the Department of Corrections. Although he looked like the hundreds of men around him, there was something different about him. He was on a journey, and it was apparent that it was a different path than his peers. *The Ride* is not about Larry following his roadmap in life, but about picking his way and choosing his path. How he went from screaming out of control on a one-way road headed to a dead-end to where he is now, is an amazing story that will encourage anyone that they also can be on a ride to success and a full life. It is a privilege, and I am honored to write this endorsement for Larry Andrews, a man once identified with a DOC number, to a man of integrity sharing his amazing story with the world. If the opportunity arises and you, as I did, want a change of course on your ride, meet Mr. Larry Andrews, and share your ride with him and let him share experiences of his own."

- Vic "Stiemy" Williams, Business Development, Halliburton
– Houston, TX; Former DOC Corrections Officer,
Howard McLeod Correctional Center – Atoka, OK

"I have known Larry for over fifteen years, and he has always been a blessing to me and to the church. I met Larry in Holdenville, Oklahoma. We were blessed with several groups holding outdoor tent revivals during the early-2000s, and Larry was very instrumental in leading praise and worship in all of them. He certainly has a love for praising our Lord and Savior Jesus Christ. But Larry, like all the rest of mankind, was not always saved. He fell in an environment of drugs and alcohol, and like millions of other people, his life went spiraling down to the point of incarceration. But the Lord Jesus Christ delivered Larry, like He delivered me and many others from all our sins and changed our lives. Larry's book, *The Ride*, demonstrates God's healing power to those who are tired of their lifestyle and want change. The transformation in Larry's life is a testimony for all who read this incredible story. Larry's life changed from a life of drugs and alcohol, to a life of serving our Lord and Savior Jesus Christ. This book will benefit many lives, and it will open the eyes of many that Jesus is our healer and our deliverer. I pray *The Ride* will be successful and identify with those who are struggling in this world, and that they will realize that God has a plan for us; a plan to bless us and to bless each other with the truth and love in the power of Christ."

Michael R. Hicks, Minister and Author, YAH
Jireh Ministries – Oklahoma City, OK

"*The Ride* is a compelling testimony in the real life story of a loving and forgiving God meeting Larry Andrews at the intersection of truth and grace. Larry's story shows us how good works done in ambition seeking honor among family and friends can deceive and trap us into believing the rules do not apply to me and we break the laws of God and men. Larry meets the truth; that law and justice demands serving a prison sentence as punishment for his transgressions. It is at this moment, when there is only the truth of guilt and no escape from the judgement of condemnation, God's gift of grace and mercy intersect with truth and forgiveness. Larry is rescued and God transforms his heart and soul, raising his spirit, soul, and body to a new life justified by faith in Christ; not justified by the works of the law, (Galatians 2), but saved to live a life of service to others and to his Lord. Larry's story, *The Ride,* will bring hope and faith to you and to those you love, especially those who feel trapped and desperate. Hear it! Share it!"

Bill Dillard, CEO, Security Solutions USA &
United Systems Inc. – Mustang, OK

"Ron Boone, an attorney friend of mine, called one day and asked for my assistance with a guy who had been to prison, but might be entitled to have his record expunged. Expungements of any kind were new to Oklahoma, one of the harshest criminal systems in the United States; so archaic it was in the top three per capita of incarceration of men, and has the dubious distinction of being number one per capita when it comes to incarceration of its felonious women. But, to expunge convictions after serving a prison sentence was unheard of.

Ron told me about this guy who had multiple felony convictions for which he was sentenced to prison. My first impression was Ron Boone had lost his legal scholar mind. But, I knew him as an Assistant District Attorney and a zealous defense lawyer. So, my second thought was, I need to see why he was wasting my time.

Ron Boone referred Larry Andrews to my law office, and Larry spun a tale that was as wild as any criminal procedure I'd ever encountered. But, what impressed me to a much greater degree was how the tale was a testimonial about the power of God when one completely surrenders his life to Him, and then proceeds to dedicate one's life to serving Him. "One" in this instance is Larry Andrews; once my new client, now my friend in Christ.

In my 35 plus years as a criminal defense attorney I can't tell you how many times I've witnessed indignant prosecutors, self-righteous cops, cynical judges, skeptical defense attorneys, and even fellow inmates, espousing a condescending refrain, "he found God in jail."

I've represented people who due to some calamity, most times of their own making, but sometimes at the hands of another, found themselves facing the gauntlet that is the criminal justice system. Whether it was capital murder, a different violent crime, a drug or alcohol related offense, there is a common denominator: Satan's Territory - that place where they or others were morally bankrupt before the arrest for violating the state's laws. So, when I hear that someone found God in jail, I pray that it's not disingenuous.

Larry Andrews has recalled personally to me his passage through what I call "Satan's Territory" to his assigned regiment as a soldier of Christ. He lives it every day. *The Ride* tells the story of a true and lasting conversion from the dark side, to the marvelous Light."

Richard Anderson, Lawyer,
Richard Anderson Law Offices – Oklahoma City, Oklahoma

"Larry Andrews' story is a life changer. I know, because it changed mine! The grace, mercy, and sweet southern kindness that pours out of this man could only come from the radical love of Jesus. But, that wasn't always the way Larry was described. The radical conversion that shook his soul and altered his eternity will blow your mind and paint the picture of what the God of the second chance can do for you or someone you love. Buckle up and get ready for ... *The Ride*!"

Lance Lang, Founder, Hope Is Alive Ministries – Oklahoma City, OK

CONTENTS

DEDICATION

To the memory of my parents, Henry and Virginia Andrews, who loved me unconditionally. They believed in me, they stood beside me, no matter what my faults were. By God's mercy, they lived long enough to see the changed man I became; an answer to their prayers.

To my wife, Kim, our children, and our grandchildren. You are blessings from God, and my life is more complete with you in it. Thank you for being there and encouraging me in this project. You are forever loved and cherished.

To my brothers, Chuck and Bruce. I love and appreciate you both.

And to my grace-giving Lord, Jesus Christ, who loved me and pursued me until I saw my need of a Savior. I thank God He left the 99 and came after the one, and that one was me. It is a debt I can never repay.

Acknowledgements

I am deeply grateful to the following for their faithful support of this writing project:

First and foremost, I offer thanks and praise to the Lord Jesus Christ, who saved me and called me to share my story of redemption and grace. I am humbled by the opportunity to serve the Lord in this way. I trust this work will be a blessing to all who read it.

To my partner and God-fearing wife, Kim. You have supported me every step of the way and provided wise counsel and loving encouragement throughout this process. You've worked alongside me in helping to build our businesses, and have served beside me throughout the ministry that God has blessed us with. You are a great mother, an awesome Gigi to our grandchildren, and a loving wife to a demanding husband. I love you.

To the ministerial staff at The Bridge, my home church, many whose endorsements are included in the book. Your prayers for me and words of encouragement came at pivotal times during the process to keep me focused on the goal of finishing and sharing my testimony. Thank you from the bottom of my heart.

To Mandy Lunsford, my assistant. You believed in the story from the beginning and spent hours making sure the manuscript flowed, facts were correct, and polished up the grammar where needed. Your spiritual insight and value throughout was greatly appreciated, but your friendship is even more treasured.

To the members of law enforcement, judges, attorneys, and correctional officers referenced in these pages. For some, we were on opposite sides of the law due to my past behavior, yet, I have found in you forgiveness, understanding, and support of this book and its ministry. I am honored to now call you friends.

Other friends and relatives too numerous to mention. You held me up in prayer until this work was completed. Sincere love to all.

FOREWORD

In this journey of life, we have highs and lows, the expected and unexpected, the good and the bad. We search for purpose, value, and the reason of our being. Who am I? Why am I here? What is my destiny? So, the search for the meaning of life continues. This is a book about one man's search; a man who had the answers; one who blazed his own trails only to find emptiness and life with no purpose, but merely existing.

Broken, lonely, and facing a possible life sentence, Larry Andrews found the answers he was seeking when he found Jesus Christ and submitted his life to God. The thrilling events that happened over the next few years of his life can only be attributed to the grace and miracle working power of a God, who once submitted to, made ways where there seemed to be no way. If you like heart-touching, uplifting, inspiring stories, you want to take *The Ride*. The journey from the dark place Larry was to where he is today is a miracle only God could perform. From the darkest of times, to the light he now lives in, is amazing. When you hear his story, you will be inspired by the grace that God so freely gives.

It has been a joy to pastor Larry Andrews and his beautiful family. From the dark place he once was, to where is he today, is a very inspiring story of his journey to God. He is a gifted singer, musician, and motivational speaker; talents he uses to touch the hearts of others. Being very involved in prison ministry, Larry is a voice of hope to those who are, or have been, incarcerated. He is an inspiration of someone who has succeeded in life after prison. Now a successful business man, Larry has spoken to not only inmates, but church and men's groups as well. As Larry's pastor, I highly recommend him as a guest speaker to any church, school, or group that wants to be touched and encouraged by his amazing story.

When you read the book, you will experience the depth of the grace that a loving, forgiving, restoring God can give. You will be touched by the change a man can make once he commits his life to Christ and seeks God's purpose. Enjoy *The Ride*.

Pastor Jim McNabb, Lead Pastor, The Bridge - Mustang, OK

INTRODUCTION

"What a ride!" - a modern euphemism for describing pleasant or unpleasant events of one's life. If the analogy holds true, the "ride" began for me and began again for me nearly 40 years later in Lexington, Oklahoma.

Headline news for 1961, the year I was born, included John F. Kennedy's first term as President, the Bay of Pigs Invasion later that year and I'll be if Russia didn't "one up" us in the space race by having the first manned spacecraft in orbit. However, the biggest news to the Andrews clan was that Virginia Andrews, with the help of a midwife, gave birth to the couple's first son on December 12th ... me.

Before it became practically a suburb of Norman fifteen miles to the north, Lexington was more a village than a town. In 1961 it was home to only about a thousand people. It is bordered on the west by the Canadian River and across the river sits the town of Purcell. A steel bridge was built in 1911 that connects Lexington and Purcell. And, here's an ironic twist. In 1971 the Oklahoma Department of Corrections purchased property in Lexington and opened a minimum security prison. By 1976 it had become a medium security prison which would figure into my personal history nearly 40 years after I was born.

Kids are either blessed or cursed with a December birthday. They either get presents from loved ones for birthdays AND Christmas, or they get jilted on Christmas because, "This gift will be both your birthday and Christmas present." I was one of the blessed ones. My parents made my birthdays special with gifts of toys, gadgets, sports stuff and then the gifts were doubled up at Christmas time; still one of my favorite times of the year.

My early years saw the family move from Lexington to Noble, from Noble to Norman, then to Washington, Oklahoma where I started school. I grew up a normal, active, happy kid until my life spiraled out of control and began to unravel.

I made some terrible choices later as an adult and seemed to be "hell bent" on destroying myself, the consequences of which seemed unrelenting and permanent. So, why am I sharing the following story about a period of my life that is sometimes difficult to even put on paper? Because second chances only come around rarely to those as lost as I was. The Lord, in His infinite mercy provided me with an opportunity to right what went wrong, to become the man He intended me to be all along, and to restore what Satan had stolen from me.

If one person reading my story is going through the most difficult trial they've ever faced; if one person grabs hold of the truth that no one is so far gone and been so bad that they have struck out with the Lord; and, if one person is encouraged to simply surrender their hearts and lives into the care of a loving Savior, then all the time, tears, and prayers poured into this effort to tell my story is well worth it.

Yes, my life has certainly been quite a ride, but there is another ride, an actual bus ride in 2001 that marked the end of one life for me and the beginning of another. One bad chapter doesn't mean your story is over. Hang on and enjoy "The Ride."

Larry Andrews
Winter, 2019

"All men make mistakes; the wise ones learn from them."

WINSTON CHURCHILL

1

THE RIDE

The wind can wreak havoc even when it isn't tornado season in Oklahoma. After a dry winter, it kicks up dust storms that sting your eyes and throat and can be especially ornery in late March. However, at approximately 4:30 on the morning of March 29th, 2001, it was dead calm.

I drew a deep breath and stepped into the cool air from the Lexington Assessment and Reception Center and shuffled toward the big green bus parked just outside the main entrance. Inmates called it "the green lizard." It looked like a normal bus, but the windows were darkened and the white letters on the side of the bus were clear even in the pre-dawn light – *Oklahoma Department of Corrections*. It was difficult to walk because my feet were shackled in irons, and I was chained to the other men, but what was most uncomfortable was the infamous "black box" that fit over the hand-cuffs and connected to the chain around my waist. The box was so tight, there was little to no movement possible for my wrists or hands. Most states would later determine that the box can only be used in the frontal position, because when used with hands behind the back, it can cause serious injury. That morning I just knew that the box guaranteed there was no way to free my hands.

There were two correctional officers aboard the bus, besides the driver. The two officers took up positions at the front and back of the bus; one facing the seated prisoners and one guarding the back. Both were armed with shotguns. I can't recall what either of them looked like. I just remember a gruff voice shouting orders as soon as the bus was ready to roll.

"At each stop we will announce the name of the facility; whereby we will call out your ODOC number (the identification number assigned to you by the Oklahoma Department of Corrections), and if the stop is your destination point, you will be escorted off the bus. We expect you to follow instructions precisely. There will be no talking; absolutely no conversation permitted between each other. All right, we're ready to go."

The bus was full that morning; looked to be around 20 plus inmates transferring to other facilities around the state. I'd been at the Assessment Center in Lexington for approximately two weeks, and I wondered if any one else was headed to Davis Correctional Facility in Holdenville besides me. I glanced around at the other men on the bus, but made no direct eye contact. You learn early when incarcerated not to stare at anyone, unless you're looking for a fight. To this day, I can't even recall what the guy seated right next to me looked like.

The bus rumbled out of the facility parking lot and on to the highway. Closing my eyes, I leaned back in the seat and thought of the disappointment in my father's voice and the pain in my mother's eyes when I last saw them. The shame I had brought on my family weighed heavy on my conscious, and I shook my head trying to erase the words my father had spoken to me a few years before, "Of all my boys, I never dreamed you'd be the one."

"The one" ... in trouble off and on for years like there would never come a day of reckoning. Now I faced a huge prison sentence, and I winced at the thought of freedom lost because of my own doing; there was no one else to blame.

Silence can truly be deafening. It was eerily quiet as we rode along with only the sound of the bus motor for company. I wondered if every man on the bus was thinking about the same things: What will the next stop for me be like? Should I be afraid? Were they praying like I was that God would show me mercy? I'm sure there were men on the bus facing hard time for murder, assault, rape, drugs … maybe even some innocent victims of the system. That certainly wasn't me; my luck had simply run out after years of *beating* the system.

I ticked off the charges in my head: Assault and Battery, Conspiracy to Manufacture Meth, Possession with Intent to Distribute Controlled Dangerous Substances, numerous weapons charges, no-show for court dates, etc. Quite a history for a 39-year-old man whom others saw as a successful business man until the media in the area got a hold of my arrest and splashed it across every local newspaper.

The charges added up to a sentence of one hundred and one years, to run concurrently. The most serious charge; what they call the "controlling case" against me, was the conspiracy to manufacture meth charge, which on its own was a mandatory minimum sentence of twenty years. I thought of that possibility – twenty years of my life – locked up. I shrugged that out of my mind. Surely God had another plan for me.

And just how did God figure into my thoughts during the ride? A month and a half before I got to Lexington, I had an encounter with the Almighty in a county jail cell that turned my life around. It wasn't one of those jail house conversions where someone uses religion to ease their guilt or hold sway with a parole board. Nope, this was a thorough, unmistakable awakening to the power and mercies of a God who finally got my attention … true salvation washed over and through me in almost an instantaneous, miraculous way difficult to explain. I was really "saved" … never to be the same again. But that story comes later.

So, even though there were uncertainties, and I fought to keep my emotions in check, there was an underlying calmness because I didn't feel alone anymore. Whatever the future held, I had a supernatural confidence that it would be God's will, and I would be happy with that.

The bus made several stops, and at some point, they announced a stop at Hominy, Oklahoma. I knew Hominy was east and quite a ways from Lexington and couldn't understand why my stop wasn't coming up sooner. Holdenville was only about 60 miles from Lexington, but of course, I dared not question the pre-determined route. Turns out Holdenville would be the last stop for the green lizard, which would make "the ride" for me about fourteen hours long, and I would be the last one off. It was dark when I left Lexington, and it would be dark when I finally arrived in Holdenville. I had plenty of time to think about how I ended up on that bus.

Every time ODOC numbers were called out, the electric door was opened by the driver and inmates were taken off the bus, but more got on, too. There are constant transfers within the system, so the bus stayed nearly full after each stop with men coming and going.

I prayed, genuinely prayed on that ride. I honestly thanked God for saving my life; if I had continued down the path I was on I would have been dead, or so strung out on drugs that I might have never returned. Using a needle was the next natural step in my drug progression, and that would have taken me to a different level. I was stopped short of forming that demonic habit which probably would have taken my life. I also thanked the Lord for a family that still loved and supported me even though I had caused them great pain.

The ride was therapeutic in many ways. But, one question kept nagging me until I cast my eyes upward and silently asked, "God, how in the world did I end up here?"

There was no audible voice, just the sense of His presence as He answered, "You are here because you were not serving Me."

Like looking out the window of a fast-moving train, I could see the years of my life flashing by, and I thought of all the wasted time I had spent without Him ...

"The enemy intended to harm me, but God intended it all for good, He brought me to this position so I could save the lives of many people," (Genesis 50:20 NLT)

*"Here's what we've learned about raising boys ...
boys will be boys."*

HENRY & VIRGINIA ANDREWS

2

HOME SWEET HOME
WASHINGTON, OKLAHOMA

I tried to cope with some hard realities on the bus ride from Lexington to Holdenville; the biggest of which was that I was staring at a long prison term away from family and friends and an uncertain future at best. So, how did the journey start that brought me to that bus, that ride, that point in life?

As stated earlier, I was born in Lexington, Oklahoma, but the first home I recall as a three-year-old was in Noble, Oklahoma; a small three-bedroom frame house with a carport, no garage. There seemed to be plenty of kids around to play with, and my brother, Chuck had been born by then, too. We are only 22 months apart. I've been told I was an active youngster, loved to have fun, also took after my dad in that I never met a stranger. Nope, not a shy bone in my body.

From Noble, the family moved to Norman where Dad operated

a service station for a time. Then came the move to Washington, Oklahoma where I started first grade in 1968.

I liked school, but was mischievous and gave my first teacher fits. Her name was Elsie Worden. Mrs. Worden gained my respect over time as she tried her best to settle me down. One time she took me to a janitor's closet, closed the door and held up a small brush and said, "I will wear your tail out with this if you don't straighten up."

I got the message, at least through the first grade. I remember, too, that her husband, Buster, brought candy for the class many times. I heard she had Alzheimer's later on and have regrets that I didn't take an opportunity to visit and thank her in person for giving me the first taste of "tough love".

Dad's work required a move to Amarillo, Texas after I finished 1st grade, and then we relocated back to Oklahoma City where I spent the 2nd grade and part of my 3rd grade year. I continued to get into trouble in the Oklahoma City school, so Dad moved us back to Washington, in large part due to my bad behavior.

I don't know exactly what it was that kept me on the edge of trouble. I seemed to be always looking for a fight or feeling that I needed to take up for someone. It could have been attributed to the fact that I hung out mostly with older kids who taught me how to fight and cuss up a storm. When I was a little older, I accompanied Dad to his various work sites. He was a general contractor, and I was around his crews who didn't put a hold on the bad language or dirty jokes just because a juvenile was present. They treated me like one of the guys, and I soon was picking up their bad language and other habits.

Dad was a little over six feet tall and an Elvis look-a-like as a young man. He kept his full head of black hair in place with Brylcreem or some such product. He could make small talk with anyone and had a great sense of humor, but when it came to discipline, he could dole it out swift and hard. I was closer to Mom as a little guy, and Dad told me I would scream whenever he even came near. But, I developed a close relationship with Dad as I grew older.

7

I found I could confide in him, and it wasn't long until I learned to respect his business sense, too.

I wouldn't say that Mom and Dad were a romantic couple. They were both reserved in their emotions, but I never remember Dad leaving for work without giving Mom a kiss. They met in 1959 when Mom waited tables at Ruby's 77 Cafe in Purcell, Oklahoma. Dad came in for coffee and a piece of pie, and before he left he had eaten almost an entire coconut pie just so he could visit longer with the pretty dark-haired girl named Virginia. He finally gained enough courage to ask for a date, but as for coconut pie, he often said he'd never eat another piece; he'd had enough. I was born a year later almost to the day after they married in December, 1960.

I knew my parents loved my brother and me, but we didn't hear the words much from Dad. Mom was a hugger and often told us she loved us, but Dad didn't express those feelings until his later years. He demonstrated his love by providing for us and buying us toys, gadgets, motorcycles, musical instruments, and the latest games. We always had the best bicycles and the finest sports equipment of any kids in the neighborhood. In fact, you might even say we were sort of "spoiled" in that regard. There was never a time that we felt deprived of anything. The only time I remember Mom working outside the home was when we lived in Noble, and Dad was just getting his business started. At some point, she started doing accounting work for Dad's contracting business, but that wasn't a full-time job.

When I was nine-years-old, our youngest brother, Bruce, was born into the family. You'd think I'd be closer to Chuck, nearly my twin in age, but Bruce and I would form a unique bond. He would follow me around, want to emulate me in every way, and even beg to sleep in my bed. I didn't mind; I saw it as the duty of a big brother to be his protector.

Mom always made sure we had a good breakfast before school and supper on the table every night. You could tell she loved to cook for us, but now, with three boys in the home, Mom would sometimes have her fill of our misbehavior. She would try to spank us, but it didn't hurt very much. When she couldn't get our attention, Dad would retrieve the belt, and armed with that tool of discipline he didn't go easy on us. Our backends knew the price for disobedience on numerous occasions.

I tried all sports, but primarily played Little League baseball and football. I gravitated toward football, mostly because it allowed me to act out aggressively; the coaches loved the fact that I wouldn't hold back on any play. Even in grade school I was always one of the hardest hitting players on the field. My love for football would carry over into high school and even college.

One thing the entire family enjoyed was music, and playing instruments came easy for all of us. I picked up a guitar when I was only four, and by age six I was playing chords. We would have a great time playing and singing, mostly country music. Mom had a beautiful voice and sang along, too.

Now and then we'd throw in an old church hymn like, "Amazing Grace," but it didn't mean that much to me personally at the time. Later, I found out from Mom that this was Grandpa and Grandma's favorite song. I discovered many years afterward that Mom had a spiritual connection to that beautiful old hymn, too.

There was no spiritual history which I can recall in our immediate family. We never talked about spiritual things, never prayed, didn't go to church, ever, except for an occasional funeral. The why we didn't do those things never came up. We were taught to not lie, cheat, or steal, and that was the extent of any moral instruction. I can't say that I was even curious about religious beliefs. I didn't ask about who Jesus was, or never registered interest in God; it just wasn't part of our everyday life. Looking back, I don't even remember anyone ever witnessing or sharing the Gospel message with me until I was older. Anyway, I didn't feel deprived; just didn't know anything else.

I truly believe Mom was a Christian. And to confirm my belief, while on the phone with me in 2004, Mom rededicated her life to the Lord as I led her through The Sinner's Prayer. She grew up in a church-going family, knew all the songs, and was a good woman who lived a very decent life. The story I recall was that her father was an evangelist/preacher who traveled around holding revivals in various churches. The religious pressure put on the rest of the family to go to church whenever the doors were open caused her to have a little "church burn out" as she got older. For that reason, or perhaps others, she didn't push us toward church, nor did she specifically instruct us spiritually, but there was always a Bible on our coffee table. I loved her; she was just a good, kind, loving woman who was a blessing to all that knew her.

Dad's family were not church-goers either; however, his mother and grandparents also kept an old Bible out in their living room that looked worn out, and Grandma Andrews certainly led the life of a believer. She and my grandparents on mom's side of the family were clearly grounded in the Word of God. There's a saying that goes, "You may be the only Bible some people ever read." I guess you could say, besides my relationship with my great grandparents on my dad's side of the family, they were the only Bible I read. I have a precious memory of playing close to our peach orchard one day when I was around 13-years-old and hearing Grandma's sweet voice singing old hymns while she sat in her recliner playing cassette tapes. Knowing what I know today, there is no doubt in my mind that my grandparents, on both sides of the family, loved the Lord.

There were 16 in Dad's family and 15 in Mom's. I had a hard time trying to figure out the names of all the aunts and uncles and a slew of cousins. We visited back and forth, but mainly with Dad's family. My grandparents on my mom's side of the family stayed heavily involved in church, but, as stated, we didn't see them as much as the relatives on Dad's side, mainly because Dad's family lived close by.

Grandma Andrews always prepared a big dinner on Sundays for all the aunts, uncles, and cousins. Most Sundays were like family reunions at her house. I did come to know and visit with family on Mom's side as I grew older.

I do think it a little strange that I never had any spiritual inquisitiveness. What little exposure I had to church wasn't good. I once attended a Pentecostal church in Washington with a friend. At a certain point in the service, people started yelling and running down the aisles, waving their arms. It scared me. I told Dad about it when I got home and he said, "Well, you don't ever have to go back there." Then, in 1972 when we lived briefly in Oklahoma City, I received a Bible from some people knocking on doors in the neighborhood. I wondered about the contents of the book, but never read it; I still have it actually. Suffice it to say, it would be many years before I would experience any sort of spiritual awakening.

Even though we were raised to have some moral character, I was just a mean kid – all the time in trouble for fighting, cussing, and leading my younger brothers astray. While I was vocal, over-confident, and brash, younger brother Chuck was a reserved kid; sort of a loner and still is. Our little brother, Bruce, was very mischievous. Like me, he liked to cuss and fight and was always up to no good. However, both Bruce and Chuck were more tenderhearted than me. Chuck was definitely more laid back than Bruce or myself. Both of my brothers were very musically talented, too.

As the older sibling, I learned the art of manipulation early and could talk my way out of trouble with Mom and Dad. I wouldn't call them total enablers, but I sure got away with a lot for which I should have been disciplined.

There were some family vacations to the lake and fishing trips. The Grand Canyon trip and Galveston Beach vacations stick out in my memory, but mainly we made short trips visiting family. In upcoming years, as I entered junior high and high school, we would travel with Dad to so many job sites around the country, that staying home was actually preferred. To this day, I don't care much for traveling and would rather be home.

In 1974, when I was twelve-years-old, Dad built us a new brick home on a small acreage in Washington, Oklahoma. It's still in pretty good shape today. The owners have taken good care of the property, but the peach orchard and swimming pool are no longer there; only the memories remain.

As normal, an interest in girls was developing as I entered junior high. I was mainly just curious about them; they were in every way different than the boys I'd hung around most of my life. They intrigued me more than anything else.

I suppose a good psychologist could see the signs of behavior that would lead to serious consequences for me later. I continued to disregard any boundary set by parents, teachers, or any authority. From grade school on, I was a ring leader for getting myself and others in trouble almost on a daily basis. If I hadn't had the interest in sports, I would have been in even more serious trouble. The participation kept me busy and focused on performing at a high level. Track and basketball soon fell away as I entered junior high, and I would concentrate on baseball and football. I loved sports, the competition, the camaraderie of the teams, all of it. Early on, coaches would tell me I had the ability to be a great athlete. That fed my ego and made me determined to prove them right.

Still, if I couldn't find trouble, I would let it find me every chance I got.

> *"Train up a child in the way he should go,*
> *and when he is old he will not*
> *depart from it," (Proverbs 22:6 NKJV)*

"Life is a matter of choices and every choice you make makes you."

~ JOHN MAXWELL

3

STARTING EARLY ON A SLIPPERY SLOPE

By the time I started high school, I had already been in a mess of trouble at home and at school; mostly for fighting. I even liked setting fires, too, but that fascination ended before I reached my teen years. As a kid, I'd light a match, then toss it out onto the grass, just for fun; to see what would happen. I have heard that setting fires and killing small animals are early traits of a serial killer; well, thank God that wasn't my destiny. I firmly believe that most of my trouble stemmed from hanging out with older boys and doing what they were doing. I wanted to be accepted as part of their crowd.

Speaking of fires, when I was around the age of five or six, Dad brought home an old car and parked it in the backyard outside the fence with a purpose of making it into a racing car. One day, I was sitting in the car with an older neighbor boy, named George, when I lit a match and let it fall to the front seat. It made just a little spark at first, but then George started trying to beat it out, but that just fanned the flames making the fire grow bigger and bigger. We had to jump out of the car and hightail it inside. Soon, I heard sirens and ran to look out the back window to see a firetruck pulling into the driveway. Someone had reported the car on fire. It was a total loss. I thought I would be in serious trouble with Dad, and I was.

There was no mistaking that Dad was upset when he got home from work that day. He always bit his tongue when he was mad or frustrated, and there he was coming toward the house, dressed in his white painting clothes, tongue between his teeth. He didn't even wait for explanations, although I was trying hard to blame it on my younger brother and George. It was one of the whippings I remember to this day.

Washington, Oklahoma, in the mid-60's to late 70's, was a town of about 600 people. There was not much to do within the city limits signs, but if you were old enough to drive, Norman is just ten miles north, Purcell is eleven miles to the east, and Oklahoma City is only forty minutes away. There was a recreation center on Main Street (actually just a pool hall) where kids would gather after school or on weekends. We had no movie theatre and no public swimming pool, so dragging Main, or just hanging out in cars parked along Main Street was just about it for local recreation. There was also a Dairy Queen on Main across from the school.

Washington had two schools at the time: one for grades K-6 and another for grades 7-12. By the time I started high school, a middle school would be added for 7th and 8th grades. The schools would accommodate a growing student population as Washington became a bedroom community to Norman and Oklahoma City. It currently is pushing over 1,000 students in the three schools.

The Warriors of Washington, Oklahoma played teams from the surrounding communities, like Wayne, Stratford, Maysville, Elmore City, Lexington, Riverside, Minco, Cyril, Rush Springs, and Piedmont. I have great memories of football games, especially during my senior year. There were only a few that came down to the wire; we usually blew other teams out of the water! We had a 7-3 record, and it was exciting to be in the state playoffs that year, facing the Davis Wolves on their home field in Davis, Oklahoma. To say they beat us soundly is an understatement. The final score was 41-8, and we were eliminated from the playoffs, but at least we made it there. The Washington Warriors would build a reputation over the years for being a tough team to beat and eventually won the state championship in 1996.

Many of my friends were already into pot by the time they reached junior high. I was in the 7th grade when some guys talked me into trying it. I hated it; didn't like the taste, the smell, the way it made me feel. I didn't care for it at all, and I thought the pot-heads I knew were really messed up. I didn't even smoke, but I would steal cigarettes from Mom to give them to my friends and watch them smoke.

The drug scene never appealed to me in high school either. I didn't like drugs or the people that did them. I tried some diet pills while playing the last football game of the season during my junior year. They gave me this boost of energy, but I also got so sick from exerting all that extra energy. I became so sick in fact, that I didn't touch those again. I couldn't have imagined the trouble I'd be in because of drugs a few years later. But, I did drink, mostly beer. We had a lot of keg parties, and it was the things we did while drinking that I shake my head at now.

Some of the friends I had in high school had been friends since elementary school. We were tight. Our senior class was very close, but there were a few, like me, who made some poor choices while others took no part in our rowdy behavior. I recall a few of those relationships, and they were like putting matches to gasoline; it was not going to be a good outcome whenever we got together. I still see some of the guys from time to time, and one of them in particular was party to my first serious brush with the law.

My buddy and I were out driving around one night and decided it would be fun to toss eggs at a night watchman sitting in a car parked outside a business on the corner of Main Street and Highway 24, right in the middle of town. We sneaked up to his car, opened the door, and threw the eggs. Mine just happened to hit the man right above the left eye, knocking his glasses off. We then took off running and hid in a trailer that was full of cotton that had just been harvested. We would learn later that the egg I threw knocked the guy out and gave him a concussion. And he wasn't a night watchman as we thought; he was a bona fide police officer.

The Washington police knew right where to find me. The injured officer saw me and recognized me as the one who walked up to his car door and threw the egg. I guess I had too much alcohol in me at the time. Besides being stupid, drinking made me really brave.

So, charges were brought against me for assault and battery against a police officer. This would be my first real life courtroom experience. At some point during the proceedings, the judge on the case took me into his chambers and asked, "Young man, do you think you could stay out of trouble for six months? Do you know what a deferred sentence is?"

I answered sheepishly, "Yes, I can stay out of trouble and no, sir, I don't know what that other means?"

He kindly explained, "Well, the District Attorney out there wants to sentence you to six months in the county jail, but I think that you didn't intentionally mean to harm the officer. Is that right?"

"Yes sir, we were just stupid, trying to have some fun."

The irony of the incident was that the egg I threw was not even a hard-boiled egg. How that raw egg could knock someone out has been a mystery to me ever since. The judge further explained that I could receive a six months deferred sentence if I agreed to steer clear of trouble for those months.

(Side note: Fast forward. I was able to thank the same judge because we became neighbors about fifteen years later. I told him how I appreciated him for blessing me with favor that day in his courtroom.) Where was God in this? Looking back, I now realize

God was trying to get my attention at different intervals of my life; if I had only listened.

I kept my word and stayed out of trouble for the most part during the next six months. At home, I tried to be good, mainly because Dad always had my attention. I wasn't afraid of him, but I knew the cost for disobeying him or Mom. At times, I think they were enablers in some innocent ways. Punishment for my behavior was swift and hard, but over too soon. I didn't really feel the consequences for my bad behavior long term. I knew and dreaded the whippings, but when they were over, it was almost like the offense never happened. I was never grounded for weeks, deprived of using the car, etc. I loved my parents, but I think they could have trained me to be a bit more responsible through those formative years.

Dad was a great help when it came to teaching me the importance of making an honest living and showing me how to deal with people. He allowed me to fail, but was always there to help me up when I did. I think he may have rescued me from consequences a bit too often. Dad was raised without much in his life and wanted us to have the best. He and Mom would do without to make sure we had everything we needed and most everything we wanted. No matter what trouble I got into, Mom and Dad were there to defend me or bail me out. I guess they excused a lot of my shenanigans with the "boys will be boys" mindset.

When I was a sophomore in high school, I had a summer job at a service station in Norman, Oklahoma. One of our frequent customers was an FBI agent named, Jim. I was always so fascinated and intrigued by him and his profession. I enjoyed a challenge, and often dreamed of becoming a law enforcement officer or undercover FBI agent one day. During one of our conversations, Jim told me, "Go get your college degree and come back to see me." Fast forward to 2001: the next time I saw Jim, he was an Assistant District Attorney in Cleveland County, and I was being escorted into the court room. We made eye contact, and he looked at me and said, "What happened to you?" I told him that my life had spiraled out of control, I had become a drug dealer, and I was being sentenced for the crimes I had committed. The look in his eyes was of great disappointment. (Side note: I went from wanting to become a law enforcement officer, to the other side of the law, to breaking the law, to running from the law, to Jesus reaching down to me in the jail cell and saving me; radically saving me. I believe this was all a part of what I had to go through to finally be saved, and I praise God for that!)

I continued through high school to always push every boundary, but I still maintained pretty good grades, stayed active in sports, and was even voted class president in my senior year at Washington High School. I even received an award for perfect attendance that year. I had natural abilities to motivate, encourage, and to lead others, but the jury was still out as to exactly "what" I would lead others to do.

A decision was looming about college. There were some football programs looking at me, so I was receiving letters of interest, mostly from out-of-state schools, and my high school coaches were encouraging me to continue playing football. I finally decided to walk-on and play for the Golden Norsemen at Northeastern Oklahoma A&M College (NEO) in Miami, Oklahoma. I fully intended to do my best, make my folks proud, and get a college degree. My stay at NEO; however, would be very short-lived.

"For I know the plans I have you declares the Lord, plans to prosper you and not harm you, plans to give you hope and a future," (Jeremiah 29:11 NIV)

"You never make the same mistake twice. The second time you make it, it is no longer a mistake. It is a choice."

LAUREN CONRAD

4

FOOTBALL, FATHERHOOD, AND FIRST TASTE

(FOOTBALL)

I was not recruited by the school, but arrived for the start of football practice at Northeastern Oklahoma University (NEO) in Miami, Oklahoma. As a walk-on player, I wanted to show them that they *should* have recruited me. I was such an aggressive player; I always wanted to be on the field going after somebody. I recall once asking my high school coach, "Why am I the only senior who is not on the receiving team?"

He answered, "Because, if you got the ball on the left side of the field and you had a straight line all the way to the goal line, but you saw one guy standing on the right side, you'd try to go over and knock him down before you scored."

I was hoping the NEO coaches saw that same determination.

Anyway, spring quickly turned into a summer that was hotter than blazes, and the stubby grass on the practice field made it seem even hotter. You could see the steam rising from our heads when we were allowed to take our helmets off, and the water breaks were few and far between. There were grueling practices three times a day.

I didn't want to be one of the many guys that dropped out during those hard days, but it wasn't just the heat that was getting to me. I was so homesick that it affected me emotionally. I would return to the dorm completely worn out and wishing I was sitting at our dinner table at home enjoying a good meal, or sleeping in my own bed. I had a girlfriend back in Washington I was missing, too; the same girl I had dated in my junior and senior years of high school. I was determined to try and make it through, but then, during a routine practice, I had a freak accident.

I was playing fullback, and we were running some drills in practice. During the drill, I got the ball, ran to my right, stiffed-armed the linebacker, and that's when the defensive back's helmet collided with the linebacker's helmet, and the tip of my left pinky was smashed off. That was it; I left the program almost immediately after. I couldn't get home fast enough.

I laid out a year and just helped Dad out; did some insurance adjustment jobs, but planned to enroll somewhere else as soon as I could. A good friend of the family, Gerald Grimes, had made me promise that I would go to college at least for a year, so that was on my mind, when once again I decided to "walk on" at East Central University in Ada, Oklahoma. I enrolled at East Central in the fall of 1981, and was sure I could be a valuable player for the Tigers. They put me at fullback, and I was enjoying the experience; not quite as homesick as before. It helped that my girlfriend's family had moved to a small school south of Ada for her senior year of high school.

Then, just as I was doing really well, during the third day of two-a-day practices, my left knee was injured, and that's an understatement. I immediately knew it was bad, because the pain was so intense I couldn't see anything for a while. I heard people talking around me, but couldn't focus to see them. The knee swelled up like a basketball.

The first surgery was performed by the team doctor and was diagnosed as torn cartilage. However, the second surgery during spring break of 1982, performed by a surgeon in Norman, confirmed that it was a torn ACL. The reality of the prognosis sunk in when I read the doctor's report indicating, "The young man is a running back, but his chances of ever playing again are slim to none." It was that bad, and I was devastated.

I was determined to play football, so before the second surgery, I made a valiant effort to report for spring practice once again. I had put on some muscle weight during the time off, so the coaches planned to move me to the defensive line because I was a strong nose guard in high school, and they thought they could use me best at that spot. My knee, however, just couldn't take the pressure of the intense practices. I would be in a great deal of pain after each session. I knew any hope of an athletic career was over. I was done.

I spent the rest of that school year focusing on my studies. My chosen major fit my aspirations, and I took courses in business management. I even took a speech class, which I thoroughly enjoyed to my surprise. The professor was encouraging as he saw that I had some "natural ability" in that area. I remember a couple of speeches that earned me an "A" for the class: "How to Pop Popcorn" and "The One Weapon I would Take if I Went to War". After everyone else chose weapons like machine guns and bazookas for war, I was adamant that the best weapon would be the Airwolf, (the helicopter known as a one-man arsenal). The class agreed that was the best weapon of choice.

(*Note to reader: If you've gotten this far in the book you have realized that God, at different intervals of my life, kept sending me signals that I needed a Savior. One strong signal occurred in Paul McGrady's dorm room at East Central in the fall of 1981. Paul was a teammate, and we both had had knee surgery, so we had something in common to talk about. During one of our conversations, Paul, a strong Christian, began to share with me the importance of a personal relationship with the Lord. Before our conversation ended that evening, he led me in a prayer to receive Christ.*

However, it was only an impulsive reaction for me at the time and not a true heart felt conversion, but a seed had been planted. As soon as we finished talking, I went to the bar, drank beer, and shot pool. I was known to earn a considerable amount of spending money shooting pool. It would be twenty years later when true conversion came to fruition, and I gave my life wholly to the Lord.

Five years after my salvation, I went to hear my friend, Bill Farley, speak at a men's prayer breakfast. While sharing his testimony, Bill asked us to think about the people that most impacted our lives; those who had had the greatest influence. Immediately, I thought of Dad, who was actually at the breakfast with me, and then, secondly, I thought of Paul McGrady.

Bill was the Athletic Director at the University of Central Oklahoma at the time and was able to put me in contact with Paul who had become the Associate Athletic Director at Southern Nazarene University in Bethany, Oklahoma. What a blessing it was when Paul and I met for lunch, and I could thank him for boldly sharing the gospel with me in a dorm room in 1981.

A few months later, I invited Paul to one of our men's prayer breakfasts where I was speaking. While sharing, I noticed him shedding a few tears when I touched on how he planted the seed that would come to fruition twenty years later. Lord, we need more Paul McGradys in this world who aren't afraid to share the Gospel and continue to live humbly and boldly before Your throne.)

Now, back to the time-line. I enjoyed my time at East Central, but in the fall of 1982, I enrolled at the University of Oklahoma. I attended OU for the first semester before transferring much later to Oklahoma City Community College for specialized business and insurance courses.

I continued my heavy drinking and partying on the weekends, and dabbled a little with cocaine, but it wasn't for me. I was living at home at that time and began to work for Dad. For twenty-plus years Dad had been the fire restoration contractor in the metro area of Oklahoma City for an insurance company whose home office was located in Dallas, Texas. There was always work available for us. I helped the crew tear out fire damaged homes, rebuild, learned carpentry, framing; even did electrical and plumbing work, too. I was a hard worker, and I was good at it when I wanted to be.

But, as was my nature, at times I tried to slide by with the least amount of effort. One case in point - we were working on the home of the family friend mentioned before, Gerald Grimes. I had been out the night before drinking and carousing. So, the next morning while others worked, I was sleeping in the dump truck at the home site with my feet hanging out the window. I didn't hear Dad pull up. He walked to the truck, jerked the door open, then pulled me out by the collar on to the ground.

He said, "If you think you are going to sleep all day then expect to be paid you got another thing coming. Now get up and get in there and get to work."

There were usually about six men on a crew; all but two on ours were family members. I was always the youngest, and as mentioned earlier, I had been hanging around these older guys since I was four years old, and learned to cuss and carry on just like them. Dad was not harder or easier on me than the others. He expected an honest day's work from everyone.

It wasn't until later that I realized that Dad had several crews at different sites. I thought that we were the only crew, but he had four or five additional crews working at all times throughout the years of doing business. That is why he was making such good money at the time. You might say Dad could be considered an entrepreneur by today's standards; he just knew the business. At one time, he had an office in Oklahoma City, but eventually moved the office to our home in Washington. That is when Mom began to take care of the payroll and all bills for the business.

I wouldn't say I liked the job, but I learned much from doing the work. I kept thinking all along; however, that there had to be an easier way to make a living, and of course, I wanted to be the boss.

(FATHERHOOD)

Around this time, I noticed a cute young woman while out riding my motorcycle around town. I asked around and found out she was a teacher at the same school I'd attended in Washington. It was her first teaching job. In fact, my youngest brother happened to be in one of her classes. So, I had him ask her if she would go out with me. She finally agreed, and we began to see each other regularly. It wasn't exactly love at first sight, but our relationship grew into love. By 1984, we had been living together for some time. She put up with my partying ways for a while, but was becoming increasingly wary of the long absences from home.

Because it seemed the right thing to do, we married in 1985. We also discovered that we were expecting a child soon. Our daughter was born in November of 1986; a beautiful little girl with lots of dark hair, dark eyes, and chubby cheeks. At first she looked more like me, then, as she grew older, she began to resemble both her mother and me. There are many times I look at her and see her resemblance to my dad.

I was elated to be a father. It seemed like an opportunity to change my life, become a responsible husband, provider, and protector of my little family. For a few months, I was home when I said I'd be home, avoided my partying buddies for the most part, and only drank occasionally on the weekends. I loved playing with my daughter, and sometimes I'd just stare at her, thinking what a perfect gift she was to us. But, old habits die hard.

(FIRST TASTE OF METH)

Within a few months of our daughter's birth, I was heavy into partying again, but took it a step further when my uncle, Dad's youngest brother, introduced me to meth. Although he was six years older, we always had the best times together. He was fooling around with meth and eventually let me try some. That was it; the high that I liked. From then on, nothing else mattered but getting that same high again and again. I don't know all the psychological and physical effects the drug causes. I just know it grabbed me like a vise and didn't let go. I didn't know at that time you could smoke it, but I knew that you could snort it or inject it. Snorting it burned my nose, and I couldn't bring myself to use a needle; just something I did not want to do, so I took the drug orally.

For a time, my uncle wouldn't tell me where or from whom he was getting the meth, but then he finally let me accompany him to a farmhouse located east of the railroad tracks in Wayne, Oklahoma. The owner operated a small business on the same property. We didn't know the rural site was being watched by law enforcement, and there were many others frequenting the place, too. The dealer was a tall, slender guy named Tommy, who looked much older than he was and usually dressed in his diesel mechanic's uniform.

Tommy was a trusting soul, and I'm sure this is eventually what got him into trouble. He gave us a choice; we could do the drugs there, or take it with us. The decision was based on how busy Tommy was at the time of the deal. If someone else was waiting to see him for the same reason we were there, to buy meth, we would take the meth and go.

Tommy had an old guitar and would always ask me to tune it for him. If he wasn't busy with other customers, after tuning, he would ask me to sing and play for he and his wife. I don't recall all the songs I played for them, but I'm sure they were mostly songs performed by Merle Haggard or Johnny Cash, such as "Mama Tried", "Branded Man", "Silver Wings", "I'm A Lonesome Fugitive", or, "Folsom Prison Blues". These are the songs I grew up playing and singing. Wow, did they come back to haunt me or what? Many years later, I had a conversation with Tommy's son and was thrilled to hear the news that Tommy had eventually given his life to the Lord.

25

My life began to revolve around meth. When could I get more? How could I get away to get it? How could I keep others from finding out how much money I was spending for it? I was making a lot of money, but wasting it on the demonic concoction that was ruining my life one dose at a time. I didn't care. I even told myself I could stop anytime; just didn't want to. By the winter of 1986 and into the spring of '87, I was spending approximately one to three thousand dollars per month on meth. So, this is when I made a business decision; I'd become the middle man for many of my buddies and start selling some of the product on the side. How stupid was that?

As with most heavy meth users, I began to lose a lot of weight. Everyone I knew began to notice, including my wife. She thought I was working too hard and excused my absences and hours away from home, telling people, "Larry is just a workaholic." At some point, I ran out of excuses for not being home and for not being a good father to my daughter, or a good husband to my wife. I wouldn't begin to count the times I concocted lies to cover my meth habit and the fact that I wasn't home when expected: I "ran out of gas," or, "the car broke down," or, "I had a flat tire." Even when I made it home, I was usually so stoned that all I wanted to do was sleep it off.

I remember one conversation my wife and I had late one night when our daughter was still a baby. She said through angry tears, "I hope you're happy. I had to borrow money from Mom and Dad today to buy diapers."

That cuts me to the core to this day. I spent money we didn't have on a stupid, selfish habit that kept me from being the father my little girl deserved. Years later, I would ask my daughter to forgive me, but at the time, I was hell-bent on doing only what I wanted to do.

Then came the conversation in the garage with Dad in 1987, when he said, "Of all my boys, I never dreamed you'd be the one."

By that time, everyone knew I was using. My youngest brother was using, too. I was shocked to find out we were buying from the same dealer.

In early 1987, I straightened up for a few months and even went to rehab. The Care Unit of Norman Regional Hospital in Norman, Oklahoma had a 28-day program. The first three or four days I slept mostly, then went to the first meeting with other patients. One by one, each would say their name and share what their addiction was. They got to me and I said, "I'm Larry ... you are all crazy, and I've got fifty cents to make a phone call. I'm calling someone, and I'm getting out of here."

My arrogant attitude said, "I'm not like the rest of you. You have a problem, not me."

I called Dad first, and he flat-out refused to come and get me. He slammed the phone down in my ear, and then I was down to my last quarter. The next call had to be a success, because my pride was not going to allow me to go back into the room with the people I just called "crazy." I reached a cousin who agreed to pick me up at the hospital and take me to Mom and Dad's home. My wife and I had already split up.

"Just don't let your dad know that I was the one who came and got you," my cousin said as he slowed the car and let me out at the edge of the driveway leading up to the house.

I entered the house and immediately saw Dad sitting in his recliner watching the ten o'clock news. A reporter's voice could be heard in the backroom as the news camera zoomed in to show a farmhouse that looked strangely familiar. A swat team in full gear had busted a guy for distribution of meth. It was my dealer. I gathered from the report that an investigation had been on-going for some time. My heart skipped a beat. I thought, "I could be next, they probably have my car tag info since I've been there so many times." I wouldn't have been surprised to see police cars pulling up to the house any minute.

I'll never forget the moment. Dad looked at the television, then looked up at me and said, "How do you like that crap?"

The words stung. Then, he got out of the recliner and went to bed, leaving me standing there shocked and fearful.

The police didn't come for me that time, but it wouldn't be long before I had a laundry list of charges against me. It didn't faze me; I thought I was invincible, outside the laws of man and God; no one could touch me or try and tell me how to live my life. "Pride come before destruction, and an arrogant spirit before a fall." (Proverbs 16:18 CSB).

I sometimes think about how God was trying to shake me to my senses. He was more interested in changing me, and not my situation. He was showing me signs of what was about to happen in my life, and the hammer was coming down. It hadn't completely fallen, but was coming down hard and fast. I just always thought it would miss me.

> *"But if you fail to keep your word, then you will have sinned against the Lord, and you may be sure that your sin will find you out," (Numbers 32:23 NLT)*

"When I'm at the bottom looking up, the main question may not be 'how do I get out of this hole?' In reality, the main question might be 'how do I get rid of the shovel that I used to dig it?'"

— Craig D. Lounsbrough

5

Finally ... Hitting Bottom

I took a breath then exploded in anger, "What the (expletive)! Are you kidding me? She cooked meth in your apartment? Get out of there! Do you hear me, get out now!"

That's how the conversation went that finally brought the law down on Larry Andrews. To reiterate, for a long while, God's grace and mercy kept me from arrest. However, a long string of charges were piling up; mostly for drugs: possession of drugs, possession with intent (to sell the drugs), DUI's for drugs, even weapons charges.

I would eventually be prosecuted and charged for multiple crimes. At the time of the incident involving the most serious charge, I was on probation for other crimes I committed. But, since I bonded out so quickly and learned how to maneuver around the system, the state could never keep me in the county jail long enough to get a conviction. I guess you could say, I learned how to manipulate the system.

When I refer to manipulating the system, there are some things I learned just from being in so much trouble with the law. For example, at random, I would hire and fire attorneys, and on one occasion, I even represented myself. For the most part, some of the attorneys would get fed up with my attitude and just ask the judge to be removed from my case. This happened more times than I care to remember. This practice of changing legal representation would cause delays, and the preliminary hearings would be postponed for two to four weeks at a time. From a financial standpoint, my manipulation of the system would become very costly. Little did I know that every time the case was postponed, the court costs were racking up. I kept the wolves at bay, so to speak, by working the system, but they would soon catch up with me.

The only thing I can reckon is that it just wasn't time for me to suffer the consequences of my rebellious behavior. God knew that I would need to get to a place where the sin in my life would break my heart, because it was already breaking His. There is a biblical reference in Romans 1:28 (NLT) about God turning some so intent on sinning over to their sins; leaving them alone to live their evil lives. It reads, "Since they thought it foolish to acknowledge God, He abandoned them to their foolish thinking and let them do things that should never be done." What a sad thing to think about. I believe that is what God allowed for a time in my life. My life had become so wild and devoid of good, that He turned me over to my sins and let me ride on that run-away train; waiting for the perfect time to pull the brakes.

By 1983, I was working for myself in the insurance business and making really good money. My first check was for $11,000, and the amount increased quickly until 1994 rolled around, and I was making nearly $40,000 a month. So, I always had money for drugs, and that enabled me and my buddies to continue in the extravagant party lifestyle.

My drug addiction wasn't so serious that it incapacitated me. I've heard of users so strung out they would kill their mother for money to get the next hit. That wasn't me; I cared too much about my appearance and what people thought of me. I was never desperate like some because I always had the money and access to drugs. Unlike most meth users, I retained my weight at around 250 pounds. Most meth-addicts look like walking skeletons with rotting teeth. The internet is full of photos of people before and after addiction to meth. Most become unrecognizable just after a few months. I was vain enough to realize that I'd start looking bad eventually, if I bowed down to the lifestyle that most addicts were living, so I made myself eat. I'd stop and get a dozen donuts and down them all at one time just to keep the weight on. This was not a very balanced diet, but it did the trick of keeping my appearance looking somewhat healthy.

Then, in 1994, an earthquake hit the Los Angeles region of California, and hundreds of insurance adjusting companies were deployed to the west coast to work as adjusters, along with contractors and general construction labor, to help restore and rebuild the damage caused by the quake. I was working for one company along with my dad and one of my brothers. We were in the area at the same time, but staying in different locations in Pasadena. I was in an apartment while Dad and many others were finding lodging wherever they could find it. After the earthquake, most apartments and motels sustained damage, so there was a shortage of rooms available.

One evening after working all day, I was walking to my apartment when I noticed the young man who leased the apartment to me in the hallway. I was sure he was under the influence of either meth or cocaine after he stopped me and asked if I had anything to eat in my apartment. So, I told him that I definitely had something for him to eat if he would give me what he was on. At first, he denied being high, but later admitted being under the influence of crystal meth.

I gave him money to go and purchase some for me. When he returned to my apartment and showed me what he purchased, I told him, "This is junk. I can't believe this is what you bought with my money!"

It looked like pieces of broken glass; that's why they call it "ice." It was crystal meth. He let me try some. I was used to taking regular meth orally, so I took a spoonful of the drug and swallowed it down. The young man's eyes got big and he stepped back and said, "Dude, you are in trouble!"

Never before, and never after, did I do anything that gave me that kind of high. This being my first experience with pure crystal meth made me think that I really *might* die. Thirty minutes later, I thought the top of my head was going to blow off.

I called my younger brother and said, "Get over here, I think I've OD'd!"

Chuck came over and tried some of the drug as well. It was awhile before he arrived, so the initial high I was feeling was starting to subside. I was definitely still high, but nothing like the initial feeling. After my brother tried some of the drug, he left the apartment to go and do something for Dad. He got lost while trying to do those errands, and this started a string of calls between me and Dad. I tried playing everything off, but Dad wasn't stupid, and he knew what was going on. Needless to say, I got an ear full from Dad for allowing this to happen. I guess you could say, misery loves company. It was many hours later that Chuck finally found his way back to the motel where he and Dad were staying. What a mess I started!

The only way I can describe it to the non-drug user is that crystal meth made me feel energetic, superior, smart, and powerful. I thought I was King Kong with a brain who could do anything! That was it. From then on I would seek that same high, that same drug, that same experience again and again. It changed something in me. There was no going back to anything which I considered inferior to that high; the highest I have ever been. I stayed wired and didn't sleep for three days and three nights from that one dose.

The biggest difference in meth and crystal meth is that crystal meth is as close to being a pharmaceutical drug as you can get. It requires a similar manufacturing process, but most "cooks" don't have the right ingredients to manufacture the pure crystal meth. You not only need quality ingredients, but all the correct equipment, which includes for the most part, a drug laboratory.

Even after the work ended in California, my addictive personality kept me making trips back to California to try and get my hands on the same powerful drug that had rocked my world. (Side note: I never experienced that same high again - ever.) I returned to Oklahoma in August, and then in the fall of '94, I flew from Oklahoma City to Los Angeles to meet with the dealer there. I was unable to make the same connection as before, so I reconnected with another dealer in the Sacramento area. The Los Angeles connection would turn out to be short-lived.

I had a decision to make during the spring of 1995, when the company I worked for presented me with an offer. I could go back to California for at least another year, or I could work in the Dallas/Fort Worth area. My wife, at the time, was so fed up with my behavior that she threatened me with a divorce if I went back to California. So, in an effort to save my marriage, the decision was made. I went to Arlington, Texas and worked for the rest of the summer.

But, the pull of the drug world and the lifestyle I tried to hide were taking a toll on every aspect of my life. While working in the Dallas-Fort Worth area, I reconnected via telephone with the dealer in Sacramento, and it wasn't long before I flew from DFW out to Sacramento to pick up drugs. Since I had no idea how to get the large quantities of drugs onto the plane on the return trip, the dealer said he would help with the process. After the sale, he said, "Watch and listen. I'll show you how to pack the meth and smuggle it onto the plane back to Dallas."

I was hesitant at first, because I knew what I was doing was dangerously wrong. It wasn't long before fear began to set in, but I agreed to follow his instructions. He told me confidently, "This is guaranteed to work."

To spare others the information they could use to transport

drugs, I will not reveal the complete packing procedure, but suffice it to say that it involves the hollow inside of aluminum cans that can easily be purchased at drug paraphernalia stores around the country; stores in my opinion that should be illegal.

So, there I was, waiting in the bag-check line at the airport while my bag was screened. I was a nervous wreck, sweating profusely and thinking at any moment security would show up to haul me out to a police car. Amazingly, there was no problem, but when the plane landed in Dallas I swore I would never try that again. For the next drug run, I drove out to California and drove back to Oklahoma with a pound of meth hidden securely in a piece of luggage located in the back of the vehicle. Normally I would drive over the speed limit, but during that trip I constantly monitored my speed to keep from getting stopped by law enforcement.

For approximately eight years, I worked for that great company out of Texas that I mentioned earlier. The owner treated me like a son. The money was great, and during a six-month period in 1994, I was making a six-figure income. On the job, I was known as an honest, hard-working individual who handled the workload presented to me in a professional manner. The owner told me I was becoming one of his main guys, and soon I'd be making more money than I had ever made in my life. Had I continued, I'm sure the salary could have led up to seven-figures.

I did a lot of things wrong during this time and was even granted a second chance to redeem myself on the job. However, my drug habits became too difficult to conceal, and soon word was getting back to the owner of the company that I suffered a gunshot wound during a drug deal gone bad. That wasn't true, but that report, along with the continued drug use, was more than I could overcome, and eventually I lost my job for good.

The truth is, I accidentally shot myself in the left hand while unloading one of my guns. And yes, I was high on meth when it happened. At this point in my life, I just didn't care about myself or the people around me anymore. My life was slowly becoming a total wreck.

It was early 1997 when my divorce was final, and about three years later, I signed my parental rights away; one of my greatest regrets. To my thinking, I was an embarrassment to my daughter, who was a young teenager at the time. I wasn't a good person and thought she needed to be free of my association and bad influence. I wasn't present during the custody hearing, but was later told what my daughter said after the hearing. My heart still aches when I think of the words she uttered to her mother when the judge awarded her mom full custody, "Dad didn't even care enough to show up and fight for me, Mom." Years later, I would deal with that recurring painful decision and ask again that my daughter forgive me. I just lost the capacity to care about anything for a time, except what money and drugs could do for me. Even losing a job wasn't a big deal because I already knew another way to make money.

I began selling drugs by just supplying my friends at first, then the circle widened quickly. By the end of 1995, I had seen how much money could be made selling drugs. I've included the information below not to "glorify" the drug business, but to inform readers who have no idea how lucrative and enticing the drug trade is to someone who doesn't care how they make money and a lot of it. I sold some quantities of pot, some Xanax, but mainly meth. One dose (a gram) is equivalent in size to a small sugar packet. This little baggie was what I called "the bell." Wave it front of a user and usually it's a sale. It sold for $100.

Many times, to increase quantities and make more money, a dealer would "cut" the meth. A powdery substance, Niacin, is often used to cut or dilute the mixture. So, instead of twenty-eight grams, the cut mixed with the meth makes it fifty-six grams to sell, etc. Most dealers take the part they want before the cut, keeping the stronger stuff for themselves, then diluting the rest.

The drug business can be very enticing. To supply my habit and lifestyle, I began to sell larger quantities of meth and would make as much as $10,000 per week. To a dealer who is also a user of the drug, the downside of the business is that drug money always stays drug money, and in the end, you are often left with nothing. Eventually, during that six-year period, my personal habit increased from costing approximately $100 per day to as much as $300 to $500 per day.

I developed the classic dealer's mentality; I loved the power and control over people. I never refused selling to anyone unless they couldn't pay me for drugs. However, on a few occasions I would feel sorry for someone if they didn't have the money to pay me, and on occasion I would give them drugs and get high with them. I also learned how to blow glass from a book I read, so I could make my own pipes for smoking meth. Sometimes I would sell someone a bag of drugs and throw in a glass pipe for free. "That's on me," I would say, like I was doing them a huge favor.

I knew that some people would bring me their full pay check every Friday for dope. My thought at the time was, *it's their problem not mine.* I would laugh with them, sometimes get high with them; never considering that I was possibly helping to deny the needs of a family or children by selling dope to parents.

I gave buyers a choice to do the drugs in my presence or take the drugs with them. If they were "tweaking out" (too paranoid, or too messed up on drugs already) I'd want them to take it and leave. There were times I refused to sell to someone who was so out of control that they could have gotten themselves and me into trouble.

"Come back when you've got some rest and your mind is a little more together," I'd say, and send them on their way. You see, drug dealers know that it isn't the stable customer, (if there is such a thing), it's the messed-up people that get you into trouble. The tweakers will tell anyone anything if high and scared enough.

Most dealers are aware that the likelihood of getting caught is increased when you are selling small quantities of drugs, like a gram at a time, to different buyers in different locations. When I started dealing outside my circle of friends, that's when my trouble really started. I didn't realize the people I was associating with outside my circle were having troubles of their own. Little did I know these people were getting charged in other counties for possession and other various charges, so the danger of being used like a pawn in a game of chess grew greater each time I sold to someone I didn't know. But the money was flowing in, and if I wanted something I found a way to get it.

I was so devoid of guilt that I saw doing drugs no worse than sitting around after dinner and having a cigar; almost a social thing. Since I had been smoking meth since the late '90's, it was so common for me and the drug crowd, that we'd hang out, pass the pipe around, and visit back and forth like it was a normal thing to do.

I continued dealing drugs right up to 2001. I knew where to get meth, and I knew cooks who made it. Some were better than others; having the right ingredients and being in the right environment is essential. I never wanted to do the cooking, but I was around when it was being manufactured and knew what went into the process. Most of the cooks I knew were hooked on the drugs themselves; teeth gone, sunken cheeks, only skin on bones, and for the most part, they were IV drug users. Thank God this is something I never did. Their homes were gone; no family, no cars, they only lived for the next high.

Eventually, I met up with a gal, Lois, who was a meth cook living in the area. Lois worked as a team with her friend, Joe, and depending on who was available, the teams were usually made up of both men and women. Both the male and the female would do what it took to get the ingredients that were needed for the manufacturing process. They would beg, borrow, and on most instances, steal from whoever had what was needed for the process. The male was normally the "cook"; however, in this case, Lois was the cook and her friend, Joe, would run and fetch whatever she needed to do the cooking. I had some of the ingredients Lois needed to cook, and she had the rest. We did a few deals together with me just being the middle man.

The month of March in Oklahoma can be harsh when

accompanied by a north wind, but it was a warm night in 1999, just around midnight, when I picked up Lois and Joe at a shabby home located on the northwest side of Oklahoma City. We drove to Norman, where I dropped them off at my friend Jeff's apartment. Jeff, whom I had known since elementary school, knew I was bringing the couple in to cook the meth. However, the plan on this particular day was for everybody to take it easy until I returned, then we would go to another location that evening to cook and complete the process.

I gave Lois and Joe specific instructions, "Lay down and get some rest. Jeff has to get up and go to work in the morning. So, you two just hang out here until I come back for you."

"When will you be back?" Joe asked.

"It will be later this evening. Then, I'll take you to a safe place to do the cook."

I had staked out a barn in a rural area that I knew like the back of my hand. It sat off the beaten path and was ideal for what we were about to do – manufacture methamphetamine.

Later that afternoon, around 4:30, I called Jeff and he asked, "Are you coming over?"

"Yeah, I'll be there soon."

"Well, bring some cut."

"What do you mean bring some cut?"

Jeff said, "She's already done; she did the cook today inside my apartment."

"Are you kidding me?" I asked with panic rising.

"No, man, we've cleaned up really well; already took the stuff to the dumpster."

I took a breath, then shouted to Jeff, "Get out of there as soon as you can. You hear me? Get out!"

You can cook meth anywhere, but it's the gassing process that has an odor like none other and is usually the tell-tale sign of meth cooking. Before we hung up, Jeff told me that his neighbor, who had known him only a short time, had already come to his door earlier in the day complaining of an odor she didn't recognize. This was bad … I could feel it; the situation had gotten out of control.

I turned to Cassie, the woman I was living with at the time. "I've got to go over to Jeff's. There could be trouble."

"No, Larry, don't go. Please, just stay away."

"I have to go. I put Jeff in this predicament. I can't bail on a friend."

I stopped and got the cut ingredient (niacin), which is used to dilute the finished product, at a local shop that sold vitamins and nutrients, along with items needed for our endeavor. I also picked up some burgers and fries, then made my way to Jeff's apartment on the east side of Norman.

When I arrived, the apartment was all cleaned up without a trace of evidence that the cook was done inside. It was clean, and from what I could tell, it was odor free, but I was still fuming.

"Lois, you've really messed up here. Give me what I've got coming, and then you guys get out of here!"

Then, I went next door to speak to Jeff's skittish neighbor. She barely peeked through the tiny crack in the door. "Is everything all right, ma'am?" I asked, smiling my best school-boy smile.

"No, it's not all right." Bam! The door slammed shut.

I was stepping back from her door when I noticed people running down the steps from the apartments upstairs. I learned later that the police had taken up positions surrounding the apartment complex and were in the process of evacuating the apartments all around Jeff's. My heart was racing as I turned to walk back to the apartment when I spotted a police car parked on the side of the apartment building. An officer got my attention from a distance and he motioned for me to walk toward him.

Trying to remain calm, I sauntered over and asked, "What's going on, officer?"

"Ah, there's a report of some kids in the neighborhood breaking into homes and scratching parked cars."

I shook my head like I knew about it, "Yeah, well, if you want to find them, they are going to be right around the corner over there," I said, pointing toward the southwest which was on the other side of the apartment complex, hoping they'd head that way.

"Well, really that's not why we're here. You are now under detention."

"Wait. What does that mean?"

"Until we know what's going on in the apartment you just came out of, we are detaining you."

I was suddenly conscious of the fact that I had seventeen grams of meth in my back pocket that I had picked up from another dealer earlier that week. "What are you talking about?"

"You know what I'm talking about," he replied.

Another officer in an all-black uniform with a badge hanging around his neck approached the police car where I was standing alongside the uniformed officer. He looked directly at me and said, "Hello, Larry, you are under detention." Once again, I heard the same words as he began to explain the difference between being detained versus being arrested. "We are going to cuff you, then place you in the back seat of the patrol car until we finish our investigation."

My first thoughts were, *this sounds like a broken record. Didn't I just hear these words from the other officer? How did he know my name? Was I that important?*

I knew what I needed to do and me being the strong willed, manipulative, deal-making man that I was, I shook my head and said, "No, sir. This is what I believe is going to happen. If I'm not under arrest and you try to cuff me, I'll resist and someone may get hurt. But, I will make a deal with you and surrender peacefully if you will go back into the apartment and bring my friend Jeff outside. He's not the one you want, it's me. When I see Jeff come around the corner of the building, I'll surrender. Then you can cuff me and put me into the car."

To my surprise, the two officers did as I requested. Now my thoughts were, since that was so easy, how can I talk my way out of this mess? When I saw the other officers escorting Jeff around the corner of the building, I noticed he was shaking from head to toe, looking like a whipped pup. That's when I held up my end of the bargain, turned around and put both hands behind my back. The officer placed the handcuffs on my wrists, opened the door to the backseat and put me inside the police car.

At the time all this happened, I wasn't under the influence of any drugs or alcohol. I got plenty of sleep the night before and was well-rested. So, even though my mind was clear, something inside my gut told me that this time I could be in some serious trouble. I didn't realize yet, just how serious. Then I thought, *Wow, they didn't inform me of my Miranda Rights. Now all I need is a good lawyer, and no matter what charges they come up with, this legal matter will be laid to rest and put behind me.*

On the ride to the police station, and knowing what was in my back pockets, I kept thinking of ways to get rid of the meth, and I was also carrying a pipe. I managed to get my hand into my back pocket, remove the pipe, and stuff it under the back-seat cushion. But, the 17 grams of meth was still in my pocket, as they led me from the car to an interrogation room at the police station.

"Thought you said you didn't have anything in your pockets," an officer said as he placed the pipe I had tried to hide on the table.

I denied having the pipe in my pocket. "Nope, that ain't mine."

Then, the officer said, "As always, the back seat was cleaned after a previous arrest, so I know the pipe is yours."

I had no answer after that news.

After the interrogation was over, I heard the officer say, "You are under arrest for manufacturing methamphetamine, possession of a controlled dangerous substance, and possession of drug paraphernalia."

In disbelief, I thought, *this can't be happening,* as the officer continued, "You have the right to remain silent …."

Could this be it? I was reminded of the '60's song, "I Fought the Law and the Law Won." *Nah, I've walked away many times. I'll beat this, too.* Then, they pulled the bag of meth from my back pocket. Hope began to waver a little, but I was still defiant and believed I'd somehow beat the system again.

A new reality began to sink in when they took us down to the Cleveland County Jail. All of us; Jeff, Lois, and Joe, were charged for several crimes, with the big one being manufacturing methamphetamine. I was in the holding tank when I recognized an attorney who had represented me on previous drug charges that were eventually dismissed. He walked over and said, "Well, what did you do this time?"

"Ah, they have me on a manufacturing charge."

"Well, you're in serious trouble my friend," and started to walk away.

I called after him, "Wait, what do you mean? I need you to represent me."

I'll never forget how he shook his head and answered, "My favors between the District Attorney and you have run out. You need to find someone that owes someone a favor. That charge carries a mandatory minimum of 20 years."

The words stunned me, and I sat there rolling the words over in my head … *twenty years … mandatory sentence.*

One of the hardest phone calls I ever made was to Mom and Dad to tell them of the arrest. To say the least, they were devastated and very disappointed, and it would be several days before I would be bonded out of jail. Jeff's brother showed up to pay his bail, and he got out immediately. I don't know if Lois and Joe made bail; they may have had to stay until the preliminary hearing. I didn't see them again until the hearing.

Just before the hearing began, my attorney leaned over and asked, "How well do you know Lois and Jeff?"

I said, "I've only known Lois for a short time, and I've known Jeff my entire life." I was puzzled, "Why the question?"

His answer was terse, "They are testifying against you today."

I could not believe what I just heard. But when the hearing

started, their testimony against me became a reality. However, Joe, Lois's meth partner, didn't testify against me. His attorney took a different approach. Not sure what his attorney worked out with the District Attorney, I just know that Joe didn't take the stand against me. But testimony from the other two was irreparable; the damage was done.

"Don't be deceived: God is not mocked. For whatever a person sows he will also reap," (Galatians 6:7 CSB)

"I saw the Light; I saw the Light
No more darkness no more night
Now I'm so happy, no sorrow in sight
Praise the Lord, I saw the Light!"

~ MUSIC AND LYRICS BY HANK WILLIAMS, SR.

6

I SAW THE LIGHT – SET-UP IN THE CELL!

I didn't blame Jeff, my friend of many years, for testifying against me. He told the truth. Can't really blame Lois either, and I don't hold it against either one of them – it was just the nature of the beast. I guess we all had a twisted way of thinking that we would never get caught. I sincerely hope and pray that Joe, Jeff, and Lois changed their lives and came to know Christ.

When Lois testified, the prosecuting attorney asked her, "Did he (*pointing to me*) ever ask you how to cook meth?"

"Yes," she answered without hesitation.

That is all it took. I didn't physically *manufacture* the meth, but I *conspired* to manufacture methamphetamine; I was guilty. That was the big one – the twenty-year sentence. This was the start of what would become several preliminary hearings according to the evidence against me. The charge for manufacturing methamphetamine was amended to conspiracy to manufacture methamphetamine, and I was eventually bound over for trial; a trial that would take place approximately two years down the road.

However; during this time while out on bond, other charges continued piling up until my last arrest in February of 2001. It was during this time the courts enhanced my existing bonds on the previous charges and increased the amounts on the bond for the existing charge to $250,000. All together my bonds totaled up to $750,000! What a mess. This was definitely the end of the road as some would say, and I can honestly say, I was tired of running. The business of drug dealing had become brutal and unforgiving. What a helpless feeling I had as the judge read his orders.

I was eventually found guilty as charged, but not formally charged until March of 2001. Between February and March of 2001, while in the county jail, I would send my attorney to the DA's office almost daily and have him try and negotiate a better deal for less time. I was desperate and out of ammunition to keep up the fight. I lacked the energy to keep going.

The twenty-year sentence seemed inevitable, but before I agreed to the 20-year offer, I asked my attorney to plead for a lesser sentence, "Try for one year."

He came back, "No way."

"Okay, try for five," I offered.

"The DA's office said that's not happening."

"How about ten – ask for ten years?"

"Nope, it's just not going to happen," he said adamantly.

I was livid, "Well, then tell them we are going to trial, and we'll fight them on every charge and drag this thing out forever."

My lawyer said, "Larry, the Assistant District Attorney, Ron Boone, said that will be fine, but what you don't understand is that *each* of these charges against you has 'life' after them. It's five to *life*; ten to *life*; twenty to *life*. Do you really want to take the chance of a life sentence should even one charge stick?"

I didn't. Finally, I accepted the 20-year mandatory minimum sentence as a plea bargain so I could have all the other charges run concurrent with the controlling case. The controlling case was the conspiracy to manufacture methamphetamine charge. The total of all charges was approximately 101 years; to run concurrent with the controlling case of 20 years.

I just kept thinking, *"How did I get myself into this huge mess?"* And I mean it was a mess; one of my own doing.

As for my friend, Jeff, who testified that I was the supplier of the dope, he got a five-year deferred sentence. Lois was given a twenty-year sentence that included ten years in the Department of Corrections (ODOC) and ten years on paper once she served the ten-year sentence in prison. She would end up spending approximately four years behind bars.

Like too many other users have discovered, meth will eventually destroy you. "The thief comes only to steal, and kill and destroy…" (John 10:10 NIV). And that's exactly what meth does. It comes upon you like a thief in the night, slowly taking away all in your life that matters.

Oddly enough to some, I maintained a friendship with Jeff, even after his testimony against me. I don't really know what became of Lois or Joe after several years. I never saw them again. As stated before, I truly hope that at some point they came to know Christ and have lived fruitful lives since.

After trying to cope with the news of the long-term lock-up, I asked my lawyer, as part of my plea agreement, to be transferred to McClain County to be sentenced on a couple of charges before I signed for the mandatory minimum of twenty years for my controlling case in Cleveland County.

I requested to be moved to a larger county to speed up the process. The term "pull chain" is used to indicate transportation from county jail to the Department of Corrections (ODOC). In the smaller counties, transportation from the county jail to the ODOC was a long wait, sometimes six months or more, and the larger, more populated counties made it easier to get on with your time because of the overflow of inmates that frequented the jail. Some of the larger counties "pull chain" and transport inmates quickly to the ODOC, sometimes daily. So, the courts agreed, and after only ten days in Cleveland County Jail, I was transferred to the McClain County Jail in Purcell, Oklahoma as part of my plea agreement and would eventually return to Cleveland County in Norman, Oklahoma to be sentenced and handed over to the ODOC.

My Dad was the strongest man I've ever known; like an old scrub oak that grows in the poorest of soils in Oklahoma. That tree survives the harshest winters and brutal dry summers. It gets twisted and gnarled from tornado force winds and rains, but somehow it just keeps hanging on and remains part of the landscape it was made from. That was Dad. He'd been through a lot, like those old oaks, but the phone call I made home to tell him that I was going away for a long time had to be one of the hardest times of his life. I should have been the son that he believed in and took pride in, but I had chosen to live a selfish, pleasure-seeking life full of the worst possible choices. I could hear the pain in his voice after I broke the news of my sentence. I know I broke my mother's heart, too.

As I was talking to Mom and Dad on the phone while in the McClain County Jail, I could hear my youngest brother, Bruce, in the background. I asked to speak to him. I knew that he was doing time on weekends at the same jail for a DUI charge, so, true to form, I told him, "Well, you know how to take care of business, right?"

He knew what I meant. I was essentially asking him to smuggle drugs into the jail for me while I awaited my return to Cleveland County. Isn't that amazing? Knowing I was eventually going to be sentenced to 20 years in the Department of Corrections, still nothing was going to keep me from abandoning my way of life. My goal and plan was to keep all my drug connections, sell drugs in prison, and upon my release, leave the ODOC with a pocket-full of money. I knew others who told me it was done inside prison all the time, so that was the plan; my mindset for the next 20 years.

Sure enough that following weekend, Bruce smuggled in the meth. He could have gotten into some serious trouble, but was only doing weekends, so I suppose they never suspected he would do anything like that.

I couldn't believe what happened next. They actually placed my brother in the same cell as me and this other guy named Sam. So, as soon as Bruce handed the meth over, we bribed the trustees with some of it so they would show us favor by giving us additional food and drinks. I took a dose and Sam, our cellmate, took a hit, too.

The next thing that happened was very unusual. Bruce didn't use that night, saying he wanted to lay down and get some rest. But me? After using, I was higher than a kite. Then, something occurred in the next few minutes that is beyond human comprehension, unexplainable, and difficult to understand. As I sat on the top bunk, I looked down at my brother who was resting peacefully on his mat on the cell floor, and something gripped my heart unlike anything I'd ever felt. A lump came to my throat, and in a moment's time, all the bad, foolish, hurtful, evil things I'd ever done loomed before me. I fought to hold back tears as a deluge of remorse washed over me. Then, I prayed the first prayer I ever prayed sincerely in my life. "Dear God," I said looking upward, "if I can influence my little brother to do something this illegal, how can I influence him and others by serving You?"

I felt a shift in the universe, a turning over in my spirit, as an overwhelming Presence filled that tiny cell. Three ultimate truths entered my soul at the exact same time: There was a God, He had heard me, and I would serve Him for the rest of my days. I didn't pray the "sinner's prayer of repentance" on that night because I didn't know how to ask. I was desperate, and knew I needed to change my life. I called out to the Lord during this time of weakness and despair. Romans 10:13 (CSB) says, "For everyone who calls on the name of the Lord will be saved." This is what I felt had happened on that February night in 2001, when I spoke to the Lord. I was saved, delivered, and set free in an instant from the addictions that had held me prisoner for so long.

I believe God saw the condition of my heart and knew I was sorry for my wretched life. He knew I was crying out to be different, better, and I needed a Savior. Wrapped up in that one simple prayer, God saw all the things I needed; things that I didn't even know how to ask for. I didn't know whether to laugh or cry. After the prayer, a sweet peace swept over me wave after wave. It was the "... peace of God, which surpasses all understanding, which will guard your hearts and minds in Christ Jesus" (Philippians 4:7 CSB). I felt loved, accepted, and clean, truly clean for the first time in my life. I was saved!

I don't know how long I felt this glorious rain of mercy, but I finally realized I was tired and very sleepy. I laid down on the bunk, turned my face to the wall, and slept like a baby for the rest of the night.

The next morning, I woke up to our cell-mate Sam, who had been high and up all night, saying, "Hey, I heard you snoring last night."

He said it like it was the strangest thing in the world. And, it was. People on meth rarely sleep; they feel super-human, very alert, and the adrenaline is on over-load. On one occasion during my addiction, I had stayed up for fourteen days straight on meth. So, to sleep soundly and wake up refreshed after using meth was part of the miracle. It was a divine covering of peace that allowed me to sleep and God's way of letting me know it was all going to be okay.

I shrugged my shoulders, "Well, Sam, I had a little talk with Jesus last night."

"Yeah, sure, you get thrown in jail, get high on drugs, and come to Jesus," he laughed.

"No, Sam, it was real, and I will never be the same ...."

Conversation was interrupted by a deputy yelling across the pod in the jail, "What do you mean you got 'em in the same cell together!" His red face told us heads were getting ready to roll. Suddenly, officers rushed into the cell and escorted Bruce to the other side of the jail. Evidently someone had figured out we were brothers. God uses ordinary people to do extraordinary things, and there's no doubt God used my brother as a vessel to get me saved. If God can speak through a donkey and a burning bush, He can speak to you through another person, while inside a jail cell or behind prison walls. I believe the Lord mysteriously allowed my brother to be placed in the same cell to be the catalyst for my conversion. I'm sure of it!

Yes, my salvation experience was unconventional. It was the Holy Spirit that enlightened me and called me in that sacred moment to Christ. I felt like the jailer in the Book of Acts, "The jailer called for lights and ran to the dungeon and fell down trembling before Paul and Silas. Then he brought them out and asked, "Sirs, what must I do to be saved?" They replied, "Believe in the Lord Jesus and you will be saved, along with everyone in your household."" (Acts 16: 29-31 NLT). Another miracle occurred that night. The desire for drugs, alcohol, and the pull of the life I had lived to that point was eradicated. I saw those things as dirty and corrupt, unbecoming for a child of God, and I never touched them again! Jesus reached down and performed a spiritual transplant of my heart, mind, and soul. That is what it was; a heart transplant! And nothing, absolutely nothing mattered except pleasing Him. I didn't just open the door of my heart to Christ, I committed my life to Him, and His great mercy and love received me just like I was.

The night I was born again opened a flood of memories to my mind and heart; there were seeds planted along the way ... the many times God in His infinite mercy had spared my life ... I recalled every gospel song I ever heard ... the Bible sitting on the coffee tables ... Grandma singing sweetly of Jesus ... a dorm room conversation about giving my life to Jesus ... God using my brother to show me the depth of my reckless and sinful life ... then gloriously accepting me, "the prodigal son," as one of His own. Knowing what I know now, I believe God left the ninety-nine and came after the one, and that one was me!

Dear God, it was for me! It was all for me! I still can't wrap my mind around such love.

It would be three years later, while in the Department of Corrections, before I would share the story of my salvation with Bruce, my brother who was in the cell that night. While on the phone, I told him how God used him to get me saved. He began to cry and weep uncontrollably and finally got the words out, "I always wanted to be just like you, brother."

The statement cut deep and caused me to reflect on the many times I did the wrong things in his sight and how the troubles he was going through might have been caused by my bad influence.

My spiritual encounter did not erase the 20-year sentence I was facing. I was transported back to Cleveland County for formal sentencing before my departure to the Lexington Assessment and Reception Center, in Lexington, Oklahoma.

The Ride on the "green lizard" to what I hoped would be my first destination at the Davis Correctional Facility in Holdenville, Oklahoma awaited me and was only days away. But, now I was a new man walking into the court room this time. I would never be alone again. God would go before me and prepare the way, whatever it turned out to be. I remember a still small voice sitting on my shoulder whispering in my ear, saying, "Sign on the line, you will never do all the time."

Just as the world has marked the years and time for ages by BC and AD – my life has been two parts:

Larry Andrews – BC (Before Christ). That one is dead and gone; doesn't exist anymore.

Larry Andrews – AD (After Deliverance). Alive in Christ forevermore! Praise the Lord!

> *"But you are a chosen generation, a royal priesthood, a holy nation, His own special people, that you may proclaim the praises of Him who called you out of darkness into His marvelous light," (I Peter 2:9 NKJV)*

"Failure is a detour, not a dead-end street."

~Zig Ziglar

7

First Stop – LARC; Human Stockyard

For the first 18 days of my sentence, I was sent to the Department of Corrections facility in Lexington, Oklahoma called the Lexington Assessment and Reception Center (LARC). LARC is where every inmate is transported for processing. It is like a distribution center, a clearing house, or closer to a human stockyard. You are processed and only kept there a short time before being transported to one of many prison facilities across the state of Oklahoma. It is sort of ironic looking back. I never would have dreamed that I would begin my prison sentence in the very town where I was born.

The first distinct memory upon arrival at the center is how the whole place smelled like bleach. Although it was March, it felt hot and sticky inside the walls with little to no fresh air flowing through. The buildings were old and run down, with concrete walls that were white-washed, yet still looked more gray than white.

Suffice it to say that my first few minutes were humbling. My head was shaved, then I was stripped to be examined for any scars or tattoos. Most humbling however, was the order to "bend over and spread 'em." I guess men try to hide a lot of interesting things in that particular body cavity. All I could think during the exam was, "Are you kidding me?" Besides underwear, they issued me a few gray t-shirts and gray pants, socks, shoes, towels, a pillow, mattress, bed linens, and the normal state-issued hygiene products. The clothing and hygiene products were a far cry from the things I had been accustomed to wearing or using. It was just one of the many times my pride would be challenged as God used everything needed to humble my prideful, selfish nature.

LARC is a maximum-security facility, and it felt like it. For the first time, I felt the stifling reality that this is what I could look forward to for the coming years of my life. It was sobering. I had heard that Department of Corrections prisons had terrible living conditions and could not compare to the private facilities across the state. I felt the sting of hopelessness that tried to control my spirit.

After being processed, I was placed in an 8x12 foot cell with another guy. There was a bunk to sleep on, one locker, sink, and a toilet in the cell. The meals were not terrible, but they weren't good either; certainly not my mom's cooking. They also got you up early, around 4 to 6 a.m. depending on your cell location, for breakfast. At 8 a.m., after breakfast, the whole place was on lock-down while they went cell to cell counting, making sure each prisoner was present and accounted for. There were various counts during the day and into the evening, as well.

For the most part, everyone kept to themselves. I didn't really want to make friends while there because, after all, I was in prison with others like me, and we didn't get to this place for stealing bubble gum. Even though I had a peace within me, I didn't trust the others around me and kept to myself, knowing I wouldn't be in the facility very long.

As it turned out, I would be there for 18 days. Even though I was only around 20 miles from where I grew up, I didn't ask Mom and Dad to make the trip to the facility to visit me. I knew my stay would be short-lived and knowing the strict rules for visitation and the many hoops we had to jump through, I didn't bother asking for visits. I did have permission to make phone calls, and I could write letters during that time, but didn't write many – maybe two is all.

I was determined to cling to my new-found faith in Christ, and discovered that Bibles were made available us. So, I requested a Bible, and I read as often as possible. My first stab at reading the Bible seriously was back when I was in the county jail, and my cousin suggested I read the book of Job. I didn't have much of an understanding for it yet, and here was this story of Job who lost absolutely everything, including his children. I remember throwing the Bible across the cell, "If my cousin was here I'd choke him to death. He knows I'm losing everything and *this* is what he told me to read."

It wasn't until later that I read the entire book, which verifies in Chapter 42, how Job got it all back and then some. Even his wife said, "Curse God and die," suggesting God had forgotten Job.

But Job's faith declared, "Though He slay me, I will hope in Him. Nevertheless I will argue my ways before Him." (Job 13:15 NASB). He knew you had to trust God in the valley as well as the mountaintop. As mentioned above in Job 2:9 (CSB), Job's wife said to him, "... Are you still holding on to your integrity? Curse God and die!"

In verse 10 Job replied, "You are talking like a foolish woman. Shall we accept good from God, and not trouble? ..." (Job 2:10 NIV)

Throughout the entire ordeal, Job did not sin; he continued to claim God's goodness. Likewise, the Bible and prayer gave me solace, and I was at peace with myself and my lot in life, but ever hopeful that my sentence would be reduced.

Imagine my surprise when I discovered that I had a cousin, Carl, who worked in the cafeteria, or what they called the chow hall, at LARC, and another cousin, Brent, who worked in the laundry facility there. Of course, we acknowledged one another, but thought if we made it a big deal the authorities might move me, so we kept the kinship to ourselves. I remember watching through the cell window as Brent moved laundry from building to building before leaving to go home. I thought, *Wow, I took so much for granted; that's what freedom looks like, and I gave it all up to chase my selfish desires.* But, I knew God was working out His plan for my life, and I had already found real freedom in Him.

It is important to note that my prayer was that after LARC, I would be sent to the Davis Correctional Facility in Holdenville, Oklahoma to participate in a program called the Therapeutic Community (TC). I believed my chances were better for a sentence modification if I were involved in such programs that were made available to train and rehabilitate inmates. While many men were court-ordered to the program; I was only recommended for the program, so I didn't know if I would be accepted or not.

When I was awakened before dawn and ordered to prepare for transfer one early morning in March, I had no idea where I was headed. I assume the destination is not revealed for security reasons. It was not until later that one of the officers let me know that I would be heading to Davis Correctional Facility in Holdenville. In my mind, knowing Oklahoma like I did, Lexington to Holdenville would be a short journey. Chained together and marched out to board a bus they called the "green lizard", I was hoping the bus was headed toward Holdenville immediately and that I would be dropped there on the first stop.

Holdenville is only about sixty miles from Lexington, so hope wavered a bit when the bus kept rolling and never turned toward Holdenville. Did the authorities get it wrong, or change their minds? The bus was heading west and then north. Quickly, I realized Holdenville would not be the first stop. I think the fear of the unknown challenges our spirits and makes us doubt God's loving care. I tried to relax during that bus ride and truly trust God with the outcome. *The Ride* was a test of my faith, and after a while, I felt a supernatural, calming peace.

After hours of travel, I fell asleep, but was awakened when the bus finally came to the first stop, the Dick Conner Correctional Center in Hominy, Oklahoma, many miles away from Holdenville. Once we left Hominy, the bus made several stops at other facilities, such as: the Jess Dunn Correctional Center in Taft, and the Jackie Brannon Correctional Center and the Oklahoma State Penitentiary in McAlester. When some inmates exited the bus, others would board. Again, I started to wonder if there had been some change in my orders, or if somehow I had been overlooked. I couldn't imagine where I was headed. By nightfall, it seemed like we were running out of stops and prison facilities. Finally, heading back toward the direction where we started, the green lizard rolled to a stop between the fences topped with razor wire, and the doors swished open to reveal flag poles in front of a white building; Davis Correctional Facility, Holdenville. I was the last one off the bus, and I now realized God had answered my prayer as I was escorted from the bus to the building. I was so relieved as the officer began to unshackle the cuffs and chains that had held me down for the past several hours.

I was tired and hungry, but so grateful. I know it sounds crazy to be happy about a foreboding place where you will be imprisoned with other men who have committed some serious crimes. I had finally graduated from the county jails to the real deal, "*prison*," and the "TC" Therapeutic Community Program was just the beginning of the many miracles God was about to perform in my life. The favor of God was upon me, and I knew He was directing my steps no matter where they led.

I didn't know what the environment was going to be at Davis Correctional Facility, how I would respond to the treatment by staff or other inmates, or what my exact challenges would be, but I knew beyond a doubt that God promised He'd never leave me or forsake me, and that I needed Him now more than ever. When *The Ride* was over and the bus screeched to a stop, my life in Christ was just beginning. I had no idea of the astounding freedom I would find in Him behind those concrete walls.

*"He was fully convinced that God was able to do
what He promised." (Romans 4:21 CEB)*

"You can kill the dreamer, but you can't kill the dream."

~ MARTIN LUTHER KING JR.

8

"DON'T LOOK PAST THE FENCE"

At one point during the bus ride from Lexington to Holdenville, I was reminded of the car trip I made with my wife and daughter sometime in the winter of 1995 or early 1996. At that time, I was making a last attempt to be a good husband and father. I had a new Mercedes, and we were traveling north on I-35 when we saw inmates on the side of the highway, picking up trash. I looked at the officers on 4-wheelers who were watching over them and made an offhanded comment. "You know, they ought to just shoot them all (the inmates) and save us taxpayers some money."

This arrogance coming from someone who had continually snubbed his nose at the law. The words came back to haunt me while sitting on that bus with others like me who were finally going to pay for their disregard for society's expectations. Proverbs 18:21 (CEB) instructs us on the importance of the words we choose to speak: "Death and life are in the power of the tongue, and those who love it and indulge it will eat its fruit and bear the consequences of their words." I was now reaping the consequences of the reckless and careless words I had spoken several years earlier.

Scripture reveals that there is great power in our words, so be careful what you speak because there will come a day when we will be held accountable for every idle word spoken. Matthew 12:36-37 (NIV) further confirms this truth: "But I tell you that everyone will have to give account on the day of judgment for every empty word they have spoken. For by your words you will be acquitted, and by your words you will be condemned."

Anyway, my arrival at the Holdenville facility at the end of March 2001 was sobering to say the least. Now it was real, and I was in prison. I was growing in my walk with Christ, but feeling some anxiety about how I was going to handle whatever was next. I knew I would be locked up with some bad men doing hard time for serious things like murder, rape, child abuse, and armed robbery. I was a big guy who had kept my body fit, so I wasn't necessarily afraid of physical threats, but I was more concerned about how my new-found faith would be tested and how I would respond to situations that could arise. But, since the night of my salvation, I owned a quiet inner peace that calmed my spirit.

I felt that God had a hand in my landing in Holdenville at the Davis Correctional Facility and that He was directing my steps. Along with many others, I would be involved in the Therapeutic Community (TC) Program for the next 12 months; a program, as mentioned, designed to teach life-skills to the many men who had made wrong choices and developed life-long habits that led to their incarceration.

I requested to be in this program hoping it would help me get back into the courtroom and be blessed with a sentence modification. For the most part, the program was very casual and peaceful, and often so laid back, I had to remind myself, *this is still prison*.

The building I was confined to was about the same size as

Lexington and close to the same design; the same concrete walls, steel doors, and chain link fences topped with razor wire. Besides the basic personal items distributed to inmates, we were issued different clothing at the Davis facility; denim jeans and button-up blue shirts. Still not the clothing I wore when I had a choice, but it was definitely better than the state-issued clothing we wore in Lexington.

To begin the day, we had group meetings, one-on-one meetings with others in the program, work assignments, and the same lockdowns and prisoner counts, but added to that was another dimension I needed very much. I took advantage of the many chapel services offered and immersed myself in the opportunity to worship and grow in Christ. As a new Christian, I needed discipleship, growth in the Word, and spiritual counseling. I prayed that God would help me become the man He destined me to be.

After Apostle Paul's conversion on the Damascus Road when he was struck blind, he traveled to Arabia, the desert region just southeast of Damascus, where he lived for three years; his training ground. He read and studied the scriptures, began to understand his calling, and prayed diligently that God would prepare him for ministry. The extent of his ministry would be so far reaching that it would eventually impact the growth of Christianity around the world.

I'm certainly not comparing myself to Paul, but Holdenville was the start of my own desert time training. I wasn't struck by a lightning bolt or blinding light, but God got my attention in the tiny jail cell with my youngest brother when I finally decided enough was enough. Now, I was hungry to know God's will for my life and eager to please Him in all things. I wanted Him to use me to spread the Word and tell others about Jesus; the Jesus who is in the business of changing lives.

I was placed in a cell with an inmate who was trouble from the beginning. He even had an issue with me doing push-ups during our 4 o'clock p.m. count, saying that it disturbed his quiet time. I reminded him, "This isn't Motel 6." We never had an altercation, and God finally worked everything out by moving me to another cell.

The opportunity for drugs presented itself right away; as soon as I got out on the prison yard. Drugs are prevalent within prison walls. The average citizen would be astounded at the business of drugs being done in prisons across the country.

Different ethnic groups controlled the sale of certain drugs; pills, heroin, pot, alcohol. You name it, and you can get it. Visitors also found ways to provide money and drugs for their family or friends doing time.

Drugs are big business in prisons across America, and as the old saying goes, "Where there's a will, there's a way" to get drugs in from outside. I've been told that drugs are often smuggled in and go undetected inside books or other gifts from visitors, and there are new ways invented every day to get drugs inside prison walls and get money into the hands of the buyers and sellers.

I clung to verses like Philippians 1:12 (CSB), "Now I want you to know, brothers and sisters, that what has happened to me has actually advanced the gospel." After I was saved, I still had to pay the consequences of my bad choices. I understood that and wanted to do my time with a humble heart and a changed attitude. I made up my mind that I was not going to continue the same lifestyle that put me in prison. I believe I was set free when I took ownership of the things I had done wrong. I stopped blaming everyone else and accepted the fact that I had lived a sinful life up until Jesus gloriously changed me. I know for a fact that God has given us the ability to change our minds, and if we put our trust in Him, He will change our hearts. All we must do is let Him do the work only He can do in us.

Mom, Dad, and others visited me in Holdenville. My ex-wife even came along for one visit, but by then our relationship was a thing of the past. I know it must have been hard on family and friends to see me incarcerated, but I was glad they cared enough to come and visit. It lifted my spirits, and hopefully they could see the change my faith was making in me.

Early in my sentence at Davis Correctional Facility, I was having a conversation in the cell of another inmate, who was serving life without parole for first degree murder. For the most part, "prison ethics" are such that you don't ask another inmate what his charges are. But, on this particular day, we swapped stories about our past life. I am not sure that this man was a believer; all I know is he had a *"gentle hardness"* about him and seemed to be someone who got caught up in the moment when he committed his crime. He explained about the fight he got into during a barroom brawl which ended with another man losing his life. Very tragic.

He asked how much time I was doing, and I told him I had a 20-year sentence. During this conversation, he said, "Look out that window." And as I looked out the tiny cell window, he asked, "Do you see that fence that's topped with razor wire?"

"Yes," I answered.

Then he continued, "If you want to be at peace and do your time, remember that life for us stopped when we were sentenced to our time. However, life on the outside continues and will pass us by for the moment."

I understood what he was saying, but being a new believer in Jesus Christ, I wasn't going to look at life that way. My mind was different, and I was at peace. The peace I felt was the God given peace; "And the peace of God, which surpasses all understanding, will guard your hearts and minds in Christ Jesus." (Philippians 4:7 CSB).

It was during this time I was reminded while signing all the court documents before the sentencing judge, of that still small voice saying, *"Sign on the line, you will never do all the time."* I truly believed God would deliver me from prison and would allow me to someday turn my *mess* into my *message* and the *test* into my *testimony*.

We casually continued our conversation before I turned and went back to my cell. Later, wondering what happened to this man, I did some research and found out that he passed away while in prison. Looking back, I wish I would have asked him if he was a follower of

Jesus Christ. Lord, forgive me for not being a better witness to this man who in his mind decided to not look past the fence.

My musical talent was an immense comfort and inspiration for me, and hopefully for others, too. I immersed myself in ministering with a praise and worship team. We had a band room where we could learn new tunes, practice, and prepare for the services. By the way, I thank God for people who are led to serve God by doing prison ministries. The chaplains, the ministers, and the laymen who give their time to speak, to pray, to share, and to counsel, make huge differences in the lives of those incarcerated; differences that may not be known until we all get to heaven. The volunteers made a difference for me, and one of my goals is to minister to others the same way. I believe we are all called to be fishers of men.

There were several pastors, teachers, and preachers from different denominations, who came into the prison and ministered to us. One such man was named, Slim, who brought the Word of God and sometimes a band with him. When he didn't have the band with him, our inmate praise team would lead the worship service before the message. Then there were lay preachers like Mitch, a successful businessman, who felt led to share the gospel within prison walls. Rhema Bible College and Victory Bible Institute out of Tulsa, Oklahoma sent teams to minister and offered Bible courses you could study to eventually earn a degree in Biblical Studies. Goldsby Baptist Church in Goldsby, Oklahoma provided me with my first Bible while incarcerated, and I still read and treasure it to this day. Prior to receiving the Bible, I was surprised by a visit from Pastor Fred Greening of Goldsby Baptist Church. He was my very first visitor in prison. What started out as strangers swiftly became a friendship, as I confided in Pastor Fred, and upon my release, served under his leadership until late 2007. It was during this time when I felt God tugging on my heart to make a move to The Bridge in Mustang, Oklahoma.

While at Davis Correctional Facility, I learned how to pray in a group, how to lead praise and worship, and how to share my story and testimony with others. I ordered Bible studies from outside sources that were made available to inmates free of charge. I used these studies as a tool to further my growth spiritually, and I came to understand that the truths I found in Scripture could be applied to everything in my life.

The prison allowed for some week-long old-fashioned tent revivals on the grounds, and they were great times of anointed preaching and worship music. During one meeting, a woman approached me, laid her hands on me and said, "God is going to use you to write many songs that will inspire people." I wish I could tell her that God indeed *has given* me some songs that hopefully will draw folks to the Lord. There are life changing truths in the songs I've written, and this book is the testament of a life that has been forever changed by the power of Jesus Christ.

One of the most meaningful spiritual experiences while at Holdenville was my baptism. They brought in what looked like just a huge bathtub, and several of the guys were lined up to be baptized that day. I remember distinctly how cold the water was – straight out of a water hose! Another inmate by the name of Harold baptized me. It's my understanding that it doesn't have to be an ordained minister; any born-again believer can baptize another. It was a blessing when I eventually had the opportunity to baptize someone, too.

The Oklahoma County District Attorney around that time was Wes Lane, whose office had declared war against meth in Oklahoma. Revealing to the public the extent of the drugs' availability and the horrific effects it was having on families and the prison systems had a huge impact. The attention ushered in new laws for obtaining the ingredients for making meth much more difficult. Mr. Lane made it a personal crusade.

In July of 2001, a staff writer for The Daily Oklahoman newspaper, Tom Lindley, contacted the district attorney's office. He was looking for someone to interview who had everything in life going for them until they lost it all to meth. Ron Boone, the assistant district attorney who prosecuted me, told him that he had just prosecuted a man who fits that description perfectly. Ron rereferred the reporter to my attorney who then contacted me for approval, and I agreed to the interview.

Lindley made his way to the prison and interviewed me for several hours inside a room with my attorney present. At one point during the interview, Lindley threw his pencil on the table, looked at me and said, "You don't fit the stereotype of a meth user." I guess I didn't look like what he imagined a user would look like; I still had my mind, my teeth and my health.

A bit puzzled, I glanced at my attorney and then back to him, "Yes, I do; look at my rap sheet."

During the interview, I bared my soul and talked about the man I once was; a manipulator, a drug dealer, an addict, a bad husband and father. I mentioned my daughter and how I had even signed away my parental rights from shame of what I'd become. But, I also added that I had hope that life would somehow be better for me now since I made the decision to follow Christ. Sure, it was a jail-house conversion, but it was real and important to me; a life changer. Naturally, the article included a reference to how many jail-house conversions go by the wayside once the sentence is served. Lindley asked, "Why should the justice system, not to mention your family, believe you this time?"

I took a moment then answered, "I think about my daughter and my mom and dad, and how I treated my dope dealers way better than I did them. I've lived this life from here to there. Out there I was a maniac. I like the life I'm trying to live now."

Lindley's article appeared in the state-wide paper on July 9, 2001 under the main headline: *METH: SHATTERED LIVES*. My featured story was titled, "Inmate Finding Hope in Life Broken by Meth". It was just one of the articles included in that particular edition of the paper. The picture that accompanied the reporter's article is included in the photo section of the book.

I made a few friends in Holdenville. In prison, you can find some good people that made really bad choices. One guy I met and instantly liked was a lifer doing time for killing another guy at a party one night. The guy said something derogatory and my inmate-friend went home, got a knife, then returned to the party and stabbed him 18 to 20 times, taking his life. I asked, "So, when are you getting out?"

His answer, "When God says its time." Even serving a life sentence without parole, he still had a window of hope that whispered, *maybe someday, I'll be free.*

I don't know how anyone makes it in prison (or life for that matter) without some degree of hope. I always remained hopeful, mainly because of Romans 8:28 (NIV), one of my favorite verses: "And we know that in all things God works for the good of those who love Him, who have been called according to His purpose."

I had an opportunity to share my testimony recently with a group of camp counselors at a foster kid's camp. I talked about this element of hope and a divine destiny. I told the group about playing football at East Central University and how I sustained the devastating, career-ending knee injury already mentioned in a previous chapter. And, how the injury led me to the dorm room of Paul McGrady, not only a leader on the team, but around the campus, who planted a seed inside me that night in 1981 by asking me about my relationship with the Lord, then, leading me through the "sinner's prayer".

I shared that it would be many years later before I would acknowledge the need for God in my life, but the seed was planted, just never nurtured. "Like a tiny acorn created to be a mighty oak tree, the acorn must be placed in the right environment or fertile soil, have the right nutrients, along with rain and sunshine, so it can establish a sound root system. Like the acorn, inside us all we have what's necessary to grow into a mighty oak tree, but we need the right elements to grow until we become fully formed in Christ. Then, that tiny acorn becomes the tree that we admire for its' beauty and strength; the giant in the forest with the capacity to withstand any weather, any storm."

The group listened intently as I testified of God's grace. "Twenty years after the seed was planted, I asked the Lord into my heart, and this time, it was real. I guess you could say, what I claimed earlier, indeed God had performed a heart transplant."

I also shared with the group that the postscript to the story is that meeting in 2006, some 25 years later, when I was blessed to reunite and have another conversation with Paul McGrady. I thanked Paul and expressed to him my gratefulness for planting the seed; the seed of hope in my life that would change me forever.

While speaking to the camp counselors, I encouraged them to plant seeds during that week of camp, because those seeds could have a lasting effect on the minds and the futures of the kids; the campers. "I also think it is important to remember that the oak tree produces thousands of acorns that eventually fall to the ground. Only a few become the sturdy, stalwart, mighty oak trees that stand as a testimony of hope; of what one may become when planted and nurtured."

I have a friend who carries a pocketful of acorns wherever he goes. When he meets someone who needs encouragement or a word of hope, he slips an acorn into their hand and shares with them the promise each acorn holds. I love that idea. It is a picture of hope.

After a few months in Holdenville, through good behavior and my commitment to be a changed man, I became a staff aide in the Therapeutic Community program. I went through the year long program. Then, in the 13th month, I knew that another change was coming, and I would soon be transferred to another facility. But, through that year, my faith grew, my Christian walk was stronger, and I knew that no matter where the Department of Corrections transferred me, the Lord would go before me.

"The Lord is the one who will go before you. He will be with you; He will not leave you or abandon you. Do not be afraid or discouraged." (Deuteronomy 31:8 CSB)

"Only to those who have been in prison, does free-dom have such great meaning."

~ Corrie ten Boom

9

FREE INDEED!

Life went on for me as I tried to adapt to life within prison walls. My hope and refuge was in God. I honestly don't know how men do time without a source outside of themselves they can call on for strength, courage, and hope. One night in May of 2002, while in my cell at Holdenville, I received word that I was being transferred to Howard McLeod Correctional Center in Atoka, Oklahoma. (I discovered later that this facility opened in 1961 – the year I was born.) Because he had spent time there, Jerry, another inmate I'd come to know, informed me that the prison in Atoka was a work camp. "Buddy, when you see the blue water tower, you have entered hell," he said emphatically.

Well, I knew that nothing on earth could be truly as horrendous as hell, but it didn't make me feel encouraged to hear him talk of his experiences there. Soon, I was cuffed and transported by van to Atoka, located near the southeast corner of the state. The town sits about 172 miles from Oklahoma City and about the same distance from Dallas. The grounds surrounding the prison cover 5,000-plus acres. An interesting fact I'd learn later is that in 1994, fourteen skeletons from four different types of dinosaurs were discovered on prison property. And yes, it was still daylight when I noticed the blue water tower right away as we neared the reception area of the prison.

I was immediately issued gray pants and shirts and assigned to a pod of the institution. I was also given work duties right away. Howard McLeod Correctional Center (HMCC) inmates were required to work in several areas: picking up trash along the roadways, cleaning out creeks, tending and growing vegetables in the large prison gardens, hauling hay, cutting firewood, and feeding cattle or other livestock. HMCC not only provides food for themselves, but other prisons around the state. We worked hard eight hour days, and my first days were especially hard because I didn't have a hat that would shield my head from the sun. Anything that wasn't included on your property list was considered contraband. If I had borrowed a hat from someone else, I took a chance that I would be written up for possession of contraband, and I was trying to maintain my level four, the highest level for good behavior. So, I just endured it, but boy, did I have a painful sunburn after a few days in the burning heat. We'd get a lunch break, usually consisting of bologna sandwiches thrown from a truck bed by the guards.

The pay for all the hard work? Twenty bucks a month when you reached level four. Four dollars would go into a savings account, and sixteen dollars went into our accounts so it could be spent at the canteen. After a few days at the facility, I called my Dad, "Well, I'm doing two things I always hated doing as a kid; swinging a weed hook and hoeing a garden."

He laughed, "Aren't you glad I taught you well?"

Within the first year of an inmate's incarceration there is opportunity to apply for a modified sentence; after that there is little contact with attorneys available. From the beginning of my sentencing I had appealed for modification, and in 2002 I did receive a reduced sentence for one of the lesser charges, but not for the one that mattered most.

While doing my assigned outdoor job of cleaning trash from the side of the roadway, I recalled the condescending statement I made years before about inmates I had seen picking up trash on the side of the road. Little did I know that just a few short years later, I would become one of those inmates on the side of the road, picking up trash. As I watched people driving their cars down the roadway I would think, *that's what freedom looks like, while here I am sitting in prison.* But, I tried to apply myself, do the best I could and maintain the highest level of behavior; a level four. You had to stay on your toes though, because you could lose your level for the slightest infraction.

After a few weeks, I ran into a guy who worked in the education program. He told me about work available in the department, so I applied to work as a tutor. Because of my college experience and good record of behavior, I got the job. The officer in charge of the program was a woman; Miss Duncan. After meeting with her, I was put in charge of the computer lab; helping inmates to attain their Adult Basic Education (ABE) and General Education Diploma (GED). I saw it as a sign of God's favor. I was able to work in an air-conditioned unit, and because of the nature of the work, there was plenty of time to read and study my Bible.

As part of their rehabilitation process, inmates were assigned to the class by the courts or ODOC based on their level of education. However, it became challenging right away because many of the guys came from backgrounds with limited education. I recall one such inmate I was tutoring became so frustrated that he flipped out, shoved the desk, and got in my face, "I'm gonna whip your tail …," he said, using a few other choice words I won't mention.

I was eventually able to calm him down after a few tense moments. I knew he was just reacting to his frustrations with learning, so I asked Miss Duncan, who witnessed the incident, to overlook his outburst and not "write him up" for leaving the class. I realized the report wouldn't help his situation or future in any way. He didn't stay in the class and was later reassigned to another job in the facility.

I did my best to teach the basics, and Miss Duncan was a good woman who understood the challenges. Many of the men in the lab completed their Adult Basic Education and went on to pursue their GED's and college degrees. I would oversee the computer lab for the next three years and never had to work outdoors again. I enjoyed the work, and as mentioned, I had time to read and study the Word daily.

Eventually, I was given one of the cubicles that line the indoor walls of the prison. Most men shared bunk beds in the middle of the floors, but these larger, one-man spaces were highly sought after. I had a locker, plug-ins, even a television set. I kept hope alive every day by reminding myself of the message God whispered to my spirit when I was sentenced, *"Sign on the line, you'll never do all the time."*

One day, while sitting on my bed in my cubicle, a young black inmate approached me and said, "I want what you have."

My first thought was, *Uh-oh, it's about to happen. This guy wants something that belongs to me and I'm going to have to defend myself.* So, I asked, "What do I have that you want?"

To my surprise, he said, "You're always smiling and you seem to be happy all the time."

Relieved I said, "Sit down here, and I'll tell you about the Jesus that changed my life."

After he sat down, we talked briefly, and I led this young man through the sinner's prayer as he gave his heart and life to the Lord. He then proceeded to tell me about being involved in the gang life and that it was "blood in and blood out," and he was concerned as to how the other gang members were going to react if he stepped away from the gang activity.

I asked him to explain his fears, and he told me how most gangs require certain things to be done as part of the initiation process and that walking away from a gang was like disowning your family and, in some cases, a death sentence. I had watched enough shows on television to know his situation could be dangerous.

After our encounter, the young man attended church on a regular basis until he was transferred to another facility. I don't recall his name or his gang affiliation, and I never saw him again. I just know God used me that night, "as a willing vessel," to get this man saved. I was so excited for this young man, knowing that God forgave him just like he forgave me. I've thought of him often and pray that his commitment that night had a positive and lasting impact on the rest of his life, and that God protected him from repercussions stemming from his decision.

Just about every night, I was in a chapel service conducted by various denominational groups. I continued also to be in the praise and worship band while at Atoka. When not playing in live services at the chapel, we had access to the band room for practicing and learning new songs. In 2003, we were very pleased to learn that our band was chosen to perform at the big McAlester Prison Rodeo in McAlester, Oklahoma; one of the most well-known and well-attended events in the state. My folks, brothers, and cousins visited me often, so I made sure my family knew about the rodeo and especially wanted my daughter to be there.

I didn't quite know what to expect, but it was a great, fun experience. We were transported to McAlester, and we prepared for the music sets. We sang and played prior to the start of the rodeo and performed instrumental tunes during the events. I sang lead and played guitar, and we had another guitar player who did some singing, too. We did mostly country tunes, but threw in some gospel when we could. I was delighted to see that my daughter did make it for the rodeo and got to come down close to where we were playing. We communicated and established some normalcy for our relationship during that visit. She came to see me a couple of times after that, and we started trying to make up for lost time.

The next year, we were asked to play again for the rodeo, but ran into some road-blocks we had to overcome. We had some great musicians in the band; the drummer and bass player were especially talented. Then, only two weeks prior to the rodeo date, the drummer and bass player were caught selling drugs on the yard. So, with only a few days left, we were scrambling to find some replacement musicians. We finally found a drummer who happened to be Hispanic, then a bass player who was Black, to add to a Native American guitar player, and me, a white guy - we were truly a "diverse-international" group of guys. We had to double the rehearsal time and practiced many long hours to be ready to perform in McAlester. We learned twenty-five songs in that two-week period, and I truly felt that God's hand was upon the group.

Just before the rodeo date, I was leaving my job in the education department and on my way to the 4 o'clock count when I checked the mail list to see if I had mail. My ODOC number was not highlighted, so I proceeded to my cubicle to prepare for the 4 o'clock count. I was surprised during the count to hear my name and ODOC number over the intercom ordering me to report to the mail room immediately once the count cleared.

The officer in charge of the mail room, Officer Vic Williams (known as Stiemy), had been assigned the duty after breaking both his wrists in a motorcycle accident. He was also known for being harsh and unyielding with the inmates, so I was apprehensive as I entered his office.

"Come in and sit down," he barked gruffly, and I obeyed. He was staring at his computer monitor for the next very uncomfortable moments. Then he said, "I really want to hate you."

I was confused, "What have I done to you?"

"It's not about what you did to me, but what you did to others by manufacturing and selling drugs. My brother battled an opioid addiction, and eventually passed away while on methadone. He fell asleep and never woke up."

I looked down and then up again meeting his eyes, acknowledging his statement.

"But," he continued, "there is something different about you. Are you coming up for parole or sentence modification soon?"

"No," I answered and waited for his reply.

"Well, I've never done this before, but, if the time comes, I want to write you a letter of recommendation."

I couldn't hide my surprise. I finally formed the words, "Thank you, thank you so much."

That was it. I walked back to my cubicle feeling God's favor once again, but we would have another conversation very soon after.

A few days had passed, and I was leaving my job and on my way to prepare for another 4 o'clock count when Officer Williams stopped me near the mail room, "Hey, aren't you going to the rodeo?"

"Yes sir, the band will be playing."

His next question caught me off guard a bit, "Who is your sound man?"

I shook my head, "We don't have one."

"You do now. I am your sound man."

"Oh, has it been approved?" I asked.

"No, *you* are going to get it approved. Go down and talk to Coach, and tell him you've found someone for the job. I do the sound for my church." (Coach was our name for the officer who oversaw the band and its' members).

I thought as he made the statement, *this is ridiculous, a correctional officer asking an inmate to gain approval to attend the rodeo,* but I did as was told and found Coach in his office, "Coach, we need a sound man and this officer volunteered," I explained.

"No, we can't do that. I don't know that we really need a sound guy." Coach took a lot of pride in the band, and he wasn't convinced we could use the help.

I was determined to plead the case, "We *do* need him. I'm singing lead, playing guitar, and running the sound. Say, something goes wrong like feedback of a microphone or someone's volume isn't adjusted properly – I have to stop playing and singing in the middle of a song to fix the issue before we can continue playing. So, having someone else on sound would really help."

He finally saw the benefit and sought the approval via phone call to the chief of security. The chief spoke to the deputy warden, who was a woman at that time, and gained the approval for the officer to travel as our sound man. She also stated, "Give Andrews what he needs." In addition, she approved the funds for musical equipment, instruments, anything we needed for the group. We were set. It was God's favor once again.

We made it to McAlester and had a great time. On the way back to Atoka, Officer Williams asked, "Boys, how long has it been since you had fried chicken?"

We all looked at each other and started answering quickly.

"Wow, it's been a while," someone called from the back of the van.

Another guy said, "Been ages for me."

I answered, "Man, it's been four years for me."

"Well, I'm going to stop and buy chicken."

We could almost taste that chicken the moment he opened the door to the van. Then, Officer Williams did something that was unheard of. He uncuffed us so we could enjoy eating the chicken. He knew it was against regulations, but he also knew that none of us were going to bolt. He even said as much. "I'm going to uncuff you guys, but just know if you run, that guy there (pointing to the officer driving the van) will shoot you."

I remember how good that chicken tasted. It was only convenience store take-out, but it was so good. I savored every bite.

It's interesting what happened next. After finishing our meal and just before we returned to the prison, we pulled off the road so that the handcuffs and the *infamous black box* could again be fastened. My shackles and handcuffs would not lock. I don't know what the problem was; we just couldn't get everything closed or locked.

Officer Williams said to me, "Well, here's what we'll do. When you get off the van, move close to me, and I will make the motion of unlocking the cuffs."

The plan went flawlessly. I appreciate this good man letting some guys like me, who missed out on so much while incarcerated, enjoy some good old fried chicken.

Recently, I had the honor of expressing my thanks to Vic Williams over the phone, and the former officer remembered every detail. He left the Department of Corrections shortly after I was released. We had an instant connection, and spoke on the phone for over two hours. We were both very excited during this conversation as we laughed about the time he fed the prison rodeo band the fried chicken. We are both serving the Lord and are both in ministry. After discussing this with Vic, I felt it was important to let the readers know there are some law enforcement officials who are decent, kind individuals with compassionate hearts, who are serving the Lord.

There were incidents of God's favor too numerous to mention during this period of my life. However, one of God's most special blessings happened one night in November when I called home to talk to Dad.

He calmly asked, "Son, are you ready to get out of there?"

"Of course," I answered, "I was ready the first year."

"No, you weren't ready then. But, I have some news. I don't know what is going on, but out of the blue, an attorney has called me. He said he's got a deal worked out to get you out."

"What?" I was stunned. "What attorney? Who called, Dad?"

"His name was Frank Snyder."

"Frank Snyder? He isn't my attorney." I knew of Snyder. He was well known in the Norman area and had the reputation of being a good attorney, but had never represented me. I was still questioning his involvement when Dad continued.

"I know, but Snyder said he had a deal worked out with the District Attorney's office to sign off on getting you out early."

My head was spinning, but hope was rising fast.

Dad continued, "I told you I don't know what's going on, but here's the phone number for Snyder, and he told me to tell you to call him. This is his cell phone number."

I took down the attorney's personal number, with the pen shaking in my hand, while thoughts ran through my head, *Could this be it? The big miracle I've been praying and believing for?* Remembering that my first consideration for parole wasn't supposed to take place until August of 2007, I was elated at how God's hand was all over this. The still small voice came into play once again, *"Sign on the line, you will never do all the time."*

We said our goodbyes, and I told Dad I would call Snyder as soon as possible. I felt like something was going on in a spiritual realm that I would never understand as I made my way to request permission to make the phone call.

Even making a phone call from prison takes some doing. I had to fill out a form noting who I wanted to call and why. I was given permission later the next day by my case manager and called Snyder's number.

He answered right away, and I listened intently while he explained what had transpired. He said, through his contacts, he had worked out a deal for an early release. There was even mention of a letter I had written to the District Attorney's office apologizing for my past behavior and testifying that my life had changed.

To this day, I do not recall writing such a letter. If I did, I have absolutely no memory of it. Could this have been a mistake? Was I confused with someone else, or was God laying the groundwork for His purpose in my life? That is what I like to think happened. It isn't a stretch for me to believe that the letter was written by someone much bigger and more powerful than me. It doesn't really matter; a letter arrived, and all I know is that someone was moved to act on my behalf. Praise God! Praise God!

Mr. Snyder continued, "Here's what I need you to do. Don't tell anyone about this yet. Give me a few months while I work on the deal with the District Attorney's office and get a court date set for you to appear before the judge. Stay out of trouble and sit tight. We will be back in touch."

My inward elation was difficult to keep secret. Just the thought that people I didn't even know were willing to fight for me and put their own necks on the line for me was humbling to say the least. And the prospect of an early release made my hopes soar. I was so grateful, that I didn't know what to do or how to act. I had to keep this wonderful news to myself while God worked out all the details.

Then, in February of 2005, I was informed that I would be transferring back to the Cleveland County Jail for court. I still wasn't telling anyone about the news of my pending release. I went to the property room to check out and to sign off on all my belongings being boxed up and held for me. The officer on duty asked, "Are you coming back?"

Since I'd been told not to tell anyone about the release, I gave a nod indicating a possible yes answer which seemed to suffice.

It seemed to happen in a matter of seconds. I was escorted through the main entrance to a waiting car with a friendly officer driving. We talked along the way and stopped for a restroom break a few moments before arriving back in Norman. Imagine my surprise when the officer took me on a leisurely drive through the Oklahoma University campus. He said, "Hey, have you seen the new changes to the stadium?"

"No, I haven't," I answered peering out the window toward the massive Gaylord Family Memorial Stadium. We drove slowly by as he pointed out the additional seating in the nose-bleed sections on the east end.

"My goodness, what people pay even to sit way up there," he mused. The university had added the seating for the growing crowds attending the OU football games. Soon, the expansion would include enclosing both end zones to create more seats. I was surprised at the changes in the last four years.

When we arrived at the Cleveland County Jail, I was booked in for the night, still not believing that by the next afternoon I could be a free man.

The next day, in the only clothing I had, (an orange jump suit I'd been assigned), I was escorted to the court room to appear before the judge with my attorney, Frank Snyder, presenting my case for early release.

And, just like that, it happened. After serving four years on a twenty-year sentence, my sentence was modified to time-served on a ten-year sentence, with the remaining ten years to be served on probation with the Department of Corrections. I could not hide the relief or the smile on my face.

Back in the court clerk's office, my attorney's partner was present. He made the comment, "I can't believe Frank is doing this. You're nothing but an outlaw, and you'll be back."

I didn't hesitate, "My life has changed, and I will never be back here," I declared. I never saw him or the other attorney again.

Dressed in the prison issued clothes, I walked out of the Cleveland County Jail toward my attorney's office where my uncle was waiting with a change of clothes. I heard later that someone had called 911 to report they saw an inmate in prison garb walking along beside the county jail and was concerned. I had a relative who worked in the county jail and had clarified that I was released and not an escapee.

My uncle and I walked out of the attorney's office and got into his vehicle for the ride home. I just kept thanking God and shaking my head thinking, *How did this happen? Only God could have done this.* The smile on my face and the joy in my heart could not be controlled. When I arrived at my parent's home, I recall how my mom cried like a baby. Mom welcomed me home like the prodigal son, and Dad arrived a couple of hours later. God is in the miracle-working business! It was true! I was free indeed. I wasn't just physically free, but free in my spirit as well. I knew God had a purpose and a plan to fulfill all His promises in my life.

Eventually, I had to return to Howard McLeod Correctional

Center to pick up the personal items they were holding for me and to return the state-issued clothing I had been assigned. The property clerk asked, "Why didn't you tell me you were leaving?"

"I couldn't tell you," I answered. I went on to explain, "My attorney instructed me to keep it quiet. I was only following his orders."

I walked out of the prison and turned to glance once more at the place I was imprisoned. For the past three years, it had been my life, but I knew in my spirit that God had done a work in me within those walls. He had strengthened me, taught me, used me, and now I eagerly awaited the next step of my life's journey. I took a deep breath and never looked back again.

"Bring me out of prison so I can thank you. The godly will crowd around me, for you are good to me," (Psalm 142:7 NLT)

"When the world says, 'Give up,' Hope whispers,
'Try it one more time.'"

~ AUTHOR UNKNOWN

10

FAVOR AND FREEDOM: THE CLEAN RECORD

All of life is made up of chances to start over. In fact, every time the sun rises, we have opportunity to re-start; to do it again, do it better, wiser, using more of what we've learned. So, it was with me on the morning after my release from prison. As expected, the biggest question on that day was, "What now?"

I knew God had protected me, blessed me with His favor, and was preparing me for the rest of my life. It was an exciting time of realizing that God had saved me for specific reasons. The new beginning He gave me was to be a testimony of His goodness and mercy and an avenue by which He would get glory. All of those things were considered as I prayed about what would be the next steps in my life.

We celebrated the night of my freedom and homecoming with dinner at a buffet where I could actually pick and choose whatever I wanted to eat; that meal was so good. My daughter had been invited by Mom and Dad, and she thought she was coming just to have dinner with them. What a moment when she saw that I was there. She was delighted to see me and to learn that I was a free man. It was a new start for our relationship, too.

The things that are taken away from you while incarcerated are things that you appreciate most afterward; driving a vehicle, the freedom to walk where you want, your own bed, home-cooking, a choice of what clothing to wear, etc. Your brain is on overload for a while just becoming accustomed to normal life once again without being told where to be and what to do every single moment. Some experts say that some inmates become so comfortable with the regimented life of prison that they find it difficult to function on the outside. Believe it or not, many who have been incarcerated for a good part of their lives re-offend, simply to get back into prison where they are most comfortable with that structured lifestyle. Not me, I relished the thought of freedom and a new start.

There were some things I needed to take care of right away, one of which was to get my driver's license re-instated. Then, of course, I needed work. My first job after the release was to work on building a steel building for a friend, Greg Quickel, who was in the construction and fencing business. Greg paid me $10 an hour.

I remember one hot summer day in July, I was down in a ditch erecting a barbed-wire fence. It was miserable as I worked, sweat streaming down my face. I stopped long enough to raise my face and voice toward heaven, "God," I shouted, "I am sick of this job, please get me a job where I can get back on my feet, and I promise I will continue to serve you." Then I went back to completing the fence.

Two weeks to the day, I received word from my uncle Nathan, who asked me to call a man I had known previously in the insurance business; Kenny Phipps. He said Kenny wanted to talk to me about a possible job opportunity connected to the Category 5 hurricane that had recently caused widespread damage throughout the south.

On August 23, 2005, Hurricane Katrina tore through the Gulf Coast of the United States and continued wreaking havoc for seven days, all the way from Florida to Texas. The devastation was monumental, and nearly 2,000 people died as a result of the storm. Images of the Superdome in New Orleans filled with evacuees left homeless still remain in our memory. I planned to call Kenny about the related job offer, but I had doubts as to whether I could work for him.

I had lost all my licenses due to the felony convictions, so I didn't think I would be allowed to work as an adjuster until the adjuster's license was reinstated. I called Kenny while attending a Washington High School football game and told him, "Thanks, Kenny, I appreciate you thinking about me, but I no longer have a license."

He said, "No, no, I don't want you to come and adjust claims; I want you to come and train the teams who will be working as adjusters. These are brand new adjusters, and you have probably forgotten more than these guys will ever learn."

I was so blessed by the offer and told him so, but answered, "Well, let me pray about it and I'll let you know."

He answered quickly, "Well, the pay is $750 a day; just how long do you think you need to pray about it?"

Remember, I was making $10 an hour at the time. I laughed, realizing what a blessing that would be and replied, "When do you want me there?" I recalled how I had cried out to God only two weeks prior and how He had answered my prayer so quickly with this offer.

Kenny's boss approved my hire saying, "Kenny, if you trust this guy, he's good with me." There would never be a question about my felony conviction, the prison time, or my past.

The blessing widened when I told Kenny that I had been working for Greg, whom he knew also from previous business dealings. Imagine my surprise when Kenny said, "Well, bring Greg along, too. We can use him as well."

The next morning, I found Greg working in his shop. "Greg, I have good news and bad news."

He stopped, put down his welding torch and said, "Okay, give me the bad news first."

"I'm quitting. I've got another job offer."

"When are you leaving?"

"Yesterday," I answered.

"You quit yesterday? Well, what's the good news?"

"I've got a job for you, too." I explained the offer and the opportunity.

So, I went from $20 a month in prison, to $10 an hour on the outside, to $750 a day doing what I knew like the back of my hand. I negotiated a deal for Greg also for $650 a day. What a mighty God we serve! Both Greg and I reported to Mobile, Alabama as soon as possible and worked for Kenny's company for the next sixteen months. Greg was my right-hand man in Mobile.

Not long after I arrived, Kenny, who got me the training job, abruptly left the company. I was confused, "You brought me on and now you're leaving?"

I'll never forget his response. He simply said, "Hang on and enjoy the ride."

He had no way of knowing that one day a book would be written, and his words would show up as the title of my book about God's work in my life ... The Ride.

Before the work assignment in the south ended, I had nearly 30 people working under me, retired Highway Patrol troopers, retired members of the Sheriff's department, and even a former Secret Service agent on my team. You tell me if the Lord doesn't have a sense of humor. The former agent and I had the same responsibilities; he oversaw another team of adjusters. We became friends, and I was led to witness to him before we left for Christmas break that December.

I returned to Oklahoma after fourteen months and worked for the same company for an additional two months from my home, at a reduced pay rate of course, but it was still very good money.

I must be transparent here. My self-image for a while made it difficult to see myself as anyone other than a convicted felon. I felt like I would most likely always be under that cloud and viewed with that label. I knew I would be okay and God would bless me, but my life and name would probably always be marked by my past. That reminded me of an old Merle Haggard tune titled, Branded Man. That is what the enemy, Satan, wanted me to believe – that I was a branded man.

The week following my release, I didn't even want to go to church. The people in the church knew who I had been and all the wrongs I had done. But after a week or so, my thinking began to change. I prayed, "Lord, I am not the same person. It doesn't matter what others think of me because You say, I am a new creation. I am not the man I used to be, the old man is dead." I began to attend church and surprisingly, the fellowship welcomed me with open arms, and I never felt belittled, rejected, or judged. They understood the scripture, "For all have sinned and fall short of the glory of God," (Romans 3:23 NIV).

Soon after my release, I joined a ministry team formed through Goldsby Baptist Church called Grace in the Trenches. Along with a praise band and some powerful speakers, we first ministered at a church in Cushing, Oklahoma and had several opportunities afterward to share. The main focus of the ministry was to challenge churches to reach out to the lost.

I continued to grow in the Lord as I embraced His Word and learned more about the power of prayer. I often sought God about needing a godly companion in my life. I dated a few women, but then in 2007, a cousin called who wanted to reach a friend he had known in school. Through a round-about way I reached the friend's sister, Kim, whom I had known from school also.

After that initial call, Kim and I had several conversations in the following weeks. She shared that she was working through a painful divorce. We met in person soon after, and as conversation goes she asked, "So, what have you been up to?"

"Well," I answered matter-of-factly, "I spent four years in prison."

"No, you haven't."

"Yes, I have." I saw the surprise as she questioned my statement. Then, when she was finally convinced that I had served time, we had a long talk about my past, but also about the changes since I found Christ.

Before our first date, Kim had spoken to her youngest brother right away after our initial conversation, "Hey," she told him, "you will never believe who called and asked me out."

"Well," he said after discovering who it was, "go ahead and see what he's like, but Kim, take your own car!" And she did.

We have laughed over that many times.

The attraction was there from the beginning. I remembered her as a cute, little, blonde cheerleader, barely five feet tall and full of energy. Now she had become a lovely, fun, and gracious woman. Most important, however, was the fact that she, too, was a believer. She had given her heart to the Lord as a youngster and was in church regularly. The foundation for us then and now is the fact that we both serve the same God who is and will always be the "Chief Cornerstone" for any relationship.

We took our time getting to know one another. She had two girls from a previous marriage, and it was important that I had time to bond with them, too. We needed to make sure that my daughter also felt comfortable with a new person in my life. She had a baby of her own by this time; my first grandchild, a bouncing baby boy.

Shortly after Kim and I started dating in 2007, I attended her church, The Bridge, in Mustang, Oklahoma. On that particular Sunday evening, there was an evangelist guest speaker. I do not remember his name, but I do remember a verse he touched on. The part I remember the most was from Esther 4:14 (NKJV), "Yet, who knows whether you have come to the kingdom for such a time as this." When the evangelist spoke these words from Esther, "For such a time as this," Kim and I looked at each other; it was as if God was speaking directly to us. The tug on our hearts was overwhelming, as tears filled both our eyes. My thoughts changed, almost in an instant, from just dating Kim, to "I believe I am standing beside my new wife." The Spirit of God was most certainly in the sanctuary on this night.

I didn't know the pastor of The Bridge, but felt I needed to meet him personally. I made a phone call to the church office and asked to speak with Pastor Jim McNabb. He was unavailable to speak on the phone at that time, so I spoke with his secretary to schedule a lunch appointment. The pastor and I met at one of the local restaurants, ate lunch, and spoke for the next two and a half hours about the church, the leadership, the pastor's vision for the church, and a little about our personal lives. I even shared my testimony with him, and he was very compassionate with his time and with the words he spoke to me, "We've all sinned and fallen short of the glory of God."

Here I was having lunch with the lead pastor of The Bridge, Jim McNabb. He had no idea who I was when I called the church office asking to schedule a meeting with him; I realize the pastor is very busy and his time is limited. So, to say the least, the impression Pastor Jim McNabb made on me that day is an understatement. He gave me, someone he had never met, over two hours of his time. I thought if he would do something like this for someone he'd never met, he is the type of leader I wanted to follow and serve under. After hearing my testimony, Pastor McNabb did not judge me by my past; he kept his heart and mind open to the person God created me to be. I have heard him say while preaching behind the pulpit, "Our church is a hospital for sinners," and, "Our mission is to help people get to the other side." Meaning, helping others go from this life on earth, to their everlasting life with our Lord and Savior in heaven. This was confirmation that I belonged in his church, The Bridge. Shortly after, I asked Kim to marry me, and I would soon relocate to Mustang, Oklahoma and make The Bridge my home church. I love my church, The Bridge, and I love this community.

After a year of seeing each other and growing our relationship, Kim and I married in September of 2008. God blessed me with a wife who received me and loved me despite my past. She has been a wonderful support and encourager, even through the writing of this book. She knows the story is an important one to tell. I thank God for Kim every day.

At the time of our marriage, I was working independently for a company out of Guymon, Oklahoma who contracted to the local natural gas company. Kim and I were able to buy a new home and closed on the house two days prior to our marriage. We spent our first night together, along with the girls, in the new house on the night of our wedding. We were all overwhelmed with gratefulness for yet another of God's blessings.

Back in 2006, I had started the process of looking into having my record expunged. I truly believe that God put it on my heart to check into it. I contacted an attorney to see what the legal process might be. I didn't even know if it was possible to have everything dismissed and own a clean record once more. But, I believed what Jesus said, "… With man this is impossible, but with God all things are possible.," (Matthew 19:26 CSB).

So, the attorney I hired petitioned the court to review my cases, with hope for a dismissal and expungement. The chief District Judge would oversee all the cases because they had occurred under his jurisdiction. There were no objections from the District Attorney's office. This lumped all the charges together and made it easier for review. I was ecstatic when I learned in December of 2006, that the judge had vacated all charges. It was a hallelujah time. A year after my release, the judge set the judgement and sentencing aside as if it never happened.

Then came another hurdle. I discovered that the felony record was still visible on the Department of Corrections and Oklahoma State Bureau of Investigations' (OSBI) web sites and records. I was deflated. How could this be? Turns out, the attorney I'd hired misfiled the paperwork and didn't include the request to have the Department of Corrections and OSBI records show the expunged sentence. In fact, he had filed everything under the wrong statute, so the public record of my felonies was still out there.

So, once again, I hired a new attorney who petitioned the court asking for an expungement of the OSBI and Department of Corrections records. Amazingly, the judge reversed his previous decision on the expungements, and records were unsealed to the representing parties. We appealed that decision to the Court of Civil Appeals in 2007, and in 2009, the Court agreed with the District Judge's opinion to reverse the expungements. A mandate was issued, and they returned the case to the District court. My emotions swung from elation to confusion. I was back where I started.

Though disheartened with the process, I was determined just to go on with my life and continue to serve God with all my heart. I knew God had forgiven me, and He knew the man I was no matter what the records showed. "As far as the east is from the west, so far has He removed our transgressions from us." (Psalm 103:12 NIV). Praise God for His amazing grace and mercy.

I continued working as a contract inspector, then in 2010, I looked into starting my own roofing business. I had a friend at the time who encouraged me to begin selling roofs for him and that helped me get back on my feet financially. I was grateful for the friend's help. Soon after, Dad encouraged me to use the experience I had to start my own roofing company instead of working for someone else.

So, the new roofing company I founded in 2010 needed a name. I felt impressed to use the number seven, often referred to as the perfect number due to Biblical references denoting completion. After receiving a phone call from a friend of mine referencing 777 as part of the company name, I prayed about using "777" somewhere in the name for the new company. Soon after, God answered my prayers when I was following a car off the exit ramp and noticed the car tag: 777. I said, "There you go. Thanks, God." Shortly after, the business was born: 777 Roofing & Construction.

Then, the next year, Dick Liddell, a longtime friend, asked if I'd ever thought of getting into the residential home-building business. He offered to finance the first two homes to get us started. To get my feet wet in the home-building business, I partnered with my cousin, Doug Hayes, on the first two homes. Doug had previously been a builder, so he would layout the procedure from start to finish, and we would work together to complete each task. Dick has since passed away, but his investment money made it possible to get "5 Star Builders" underway, the other business we founded. I needed a learning curve to grasp the financial part of the construction business, but soon I was dealing with vendors, banks, and partners in development. God blessed those first efforts of owning and operating my own businesses.

Life went on, but death visited our family, too. In September 2012, Dad passed away from congestive heart failure. He had been having heart problems for several years, even had a triple bypass, but at the age of 70, he entered the hospital again. During the next three months, he would frequent the hospital, and I visited often. On the night of his passing I stopped by again. It was a Wednesday evening around 5 p.m., and I planned to make it to church after our visit. He was lucid and communicating well. We finished some paperwork, and when I turned to go, he stopped me and said, "I love you, son, and I'll see you tomorrow." Those were his last words spoken to me.

The call from Mom to my cell phone came while we were in church that same evening around 7:20 p.m. She managed to tell me, through tears, that Dad had suffered a major heart attack and was in full cardiac arrest with minimal hope of recovery. Kim and I left church and headed toward the Norman Regional Hospital, where he had already been placed on life support. I had the unenviable position of deciding when to turn the machines off that kept his heart beating. After speaking to the doctor, we followed Dad's wish through the paper work he had signed indicating he did not want to be kept on life support. I held Dad's hand and he held mine while the doctor slowly disconnected the machines. I heard a long beep, and I looked at the monitor showing a flat line; then, I felt the grip of my Dad's hand slowly release from mine. My strong, wise, affable, caring Dad was gone from our presence, but instantly in heaven.

I knew Dad had made a decision to follow Christ years before. It was soon after his diagnosis for diabetes that he talked about eternal matters with Pastor Fred Greening, my first visitor in prison, and had claimed Christ as His Savior. I was also deeply grateful that he had lived to see my life turned completely around. Thanks to Christ, I had come a long way from the night when Dad, heavy with disappointment over the grief I'd caused, told me, "Of all my boys, I never dreamed you'd be the one." So, I knew he was proud of the man God was teaching me to be.

The funeral service was held at the church my Mom and Dad attended, and I sang one of his favorite hymns, Amazing Grace. We laid Dad to rest in the cemetery in Washington, Oklahoma with a tombstone that noted the scripture from II Timothy 4:7 (NIV), "I have fought the good fight, I have finished the race, I have kept the faith." I still miss him greatly.

Then, later that same year, Mom fell down the steps leading into her garage and broke her leg. She called one night around midnight sounding strange, "Larry, I've broken my leg."

I answered quickly, "How do you know it's broken, Mom?"

"Because it is folded up behind me." It was indeed a bad break.

During recovery from surgery following that injury, she was diagnosed with lung disease; COPD. For the next five years, Mom would struggle with difficulties breathing and coping with related problems. She grew very tired of the physical battles and would often say that she was ready to go and be with the Lord; she already had the legal paperwork in order denying any type of life support. On a night in December 2017, I sat in her hospital room, surrounded by other family members. I held Mom's hand as she slowly took her last breath, and a tear rolled down her cheek. My cousin, who is a nurse, told me, "That tear represents your mother telling you goodbye."

We buried Mom next to Dad in the Washington Cemetery. I was unable to hold back the tears while driving from the cemetery, with the knowledge that two people who loved me despite the pain I caused, and who had done their best to teach me right from wrong, were now gone. On occasion, thoughts of my parents still bring tears to my eyes. But, knowing they had committed their lives to Jesus Christ, I also know there will be a day of reunion in heaven, and when I see them next, they will be whole and happy and at peace forevermore.

Kim and I have had the same struggles many blended families experience. Raising children who are not your biological children can be difficult at times. Lines become blurred, and it takes prayer and wisdom to discipline or set expectations in those circumstances. One of the girls is now a teenager, so all the angst that comes with that period of life figures in, too. Kim and I also took on the responsibility of raising our granddaughter with all the challenges that presented. But, God has guided, and we have done the best we know to do, admitting that we are not always perfect. I have made mistakes with parenting, but continue to love and care for my step-daughters, as well as my own daughter and grandson. I pray daily that they all keep following Christ and realize His great plan for their lives.

In 2015, while on the computer, a pop-up note appeared on the site I was viewing. It read, Are you entitled to an expungement? It got my attention, and I asked myself, "Could it still be possible? Would I ever have a clean record?" It wasn't until March of the next year, 2016, when I made contact with yet another attorney in that regard.

Ron Boone, the former assistant district attorney who prosecuted me, was now in private practice as a defense attorney and had become my friend. Ron referred me to Attorney Richard Anderson's office, located in Oklahoma City. As I explained the entire situation, Richard listened attentively before he replied, leaning back in his chair, "This is nothing short of miraculous. I would encourage you to go home, print and save everything off the internet that pertains to your cases."

"Why do I need to do that?" I asked.

"Because you are going to need them for your book. I have been practicing law for over thirty years, and I am 99.9% sure if what you're telling me is true, it's a done deal."

I asked, "Well, why aren't you 100% sure?"

He replied, "Because, law is a practice whereby anything can happen in the courts."

But, Richard's initial positive response gave me a renewed sense of hope, and I felt God's hand as we moved again through the process of expungement. I had been through a unique testing time since 2006, and now all the waiting, prayer, and faithfulness to God's will was not in vain.

By the way, isn't waiting the hardest thing to do, even for a believer? God isn't saying, yes or no, He just says, "Wait." But what or who are we waiting for? You see, I came to realize that for almost ten years I had been waiting for the attorneys I had hired to get it right, or waiting on judges who reviewed my case, or waiting for the laws to change. Applying scripture, I saw that I had actually been waiting on the Lord to move in His perfect time. My perspective was altered, and I had a new peace when I saw that He had a perfect plan and perfect timing for answering my prayers. As I waited, God, all along was "... causing everything to work together for my good, according to His purpose." (Romans 8:28 NLT)

And what benefit is there in waiting? Scripture is clear; the greatest work of all could be happening in us as we wait on the Lord. "But those who wait on the Lord shall renew their strength. They shall mount up with wings like eagles. They shall run and not be weary, they shall walk and not faint," (Isaiah 40:31 NKJV).

Once more, my case was presented to the courts in Cleveland and McClain counties. In August of 2017, everything seemed to change in a matter of moments. The judges reviewing my cases ordered the records be expunged. The Department of Corrections and OSBI records were expunged shortly afterward by the orders of the same judges. I will never forget attorney Richard Anderson, leaning down to tell me emphatically, "You are expunged!"

It was done. Like Jesus said on the cross, "It is finished." Job

13:18 (NLT) confirms what I had been striving for, "I have prepared my case; I will be proved innocent."

I don't know how to express the joy I felt. It was as if God took a giant eraser and just erased the deeds, all the labels, and the past that once held me bound. I wanted to cry, laugh, be quiet, shout it from the rooftops, jump up and down, but mainly I felt an overwhelming inner peace.

That part of my journey, that chapter of my life, that part of The Ride was over. I poured my heart out to God in gratefulness. My family and I celebrated. We knew it was God's mercy that had worked the miracle. Tears came to my eyes the first time I opened the public records after the declaration of expungement and saw that the awful mugshots that had stared back at me for so many years were gone. Praise God from who all blessings flow!

Was life smooth sailing from then on? No. Were there other mountains I would pray to be removed? Yes. Was I a perfect saint, never missing a step? No, I have failed the Lord many times, but He never gives up on me.

We had particularly tough years in the business over the last few years. Roofing jobs depend on customers needing repairs after storms and bad weather. Usually tornadoes, high winds, and hail are prevalent in the Sooner state, but during those years there were no big storms that caused damage on a major scale. Not that I pray that we have storms or that people suffer damage to their homes. I'm just recounting that those results produce a need for roof repair, and that is a big chunk of our business. The economy was tight, too. So much so, that people were not making big investments on new roofs, on construction projects, or new homes. They were holding on to any money they had while the economy was unstable.

We took it to the Lord and asked Him to help us through that difficult financial period. I will always believe that giving or tithing is a responsibility and a blessing to the believer. Even while in prison, I would send monthly tithes; $2 out of my $20 pay check. I was adamant when I told Kim and office staff during that downturn,

"This is not an option. Paying tithes will come first, even if it is a sacrifice to give, we have to be obedient." And as He does, He brought us through.

The Ride for me has been a journey I wanted to document for three strong reasons. First and foremost, I wanted to glorify God by writing about a life that was so in bondage, that I didn't care that I was leading others down that same path of destruction. It took a miracle, in the McClain County Jail, to shake me into repentance once and for all. My point is that there is no one, not one person, so lost, so hopeless, that God's grace can't reach.

Second, this book is a message to believers. Don't give up on those who have disappointed you by their poor choices or lifestyle. I firmly believe I was saved because someone cared enough to pray for me. Pray, and keep praying for those outside of Christ, or those who need encouragement. Life is hard, and I keep that in mind as I go about my days. It is not unusual for me to ask to pray with someone at the very moment I sense they need it, right there, wherever it is. Won't it be wonderful when we get to heaven and see those there whom we prayed and lifted up to the Lord? You may never know how or in whom you have planted an acorn, that seed of the Gospel. But God keeps account.

Be a bold witness of God's mercy, whether at the coffee shop, the grocery store, the office, the school, and, yes, even in prison. Be strong in the Lord, and He will give you courage to confront the lost; but always do it in love. Someone, somewhere is needing to hear the good news that God loves them, sent His Son to die for them, and is coming back for His own. You be the one. "But I consider my life of no value to myself; my purpose is to finish my course and the ministry I received from the Lord Jesus, to testify to the gospel of God's grace." (Acts 20:24 CSB).

Then, thirdly, this book is a reminder to please God alone. Stay faithful, even when others doubt your conversion or your walk with God. So many people, those in law enforcement, attorneys, other inmates, church members, even a few in my own family didn't give much credence to my commitment to the Lord.

"Just wait, you'll see. The first real hard time comes, and Larry will once more turn to drugs," some would say. Or, "He's just using a jail house confession to gain favor toward parole; we'll see if it lasts when he's a free man." And this, "I hope he makes it, but he's been pretty bad; don't know if he can truly be a new person; too much baggage."

They are right in some respects. I cannot stand, persevere, grow in Christ, or stay committed on my own. Often the greatest battle for peace is the one that happens inside of us. There is a story, of unknown origin, of a grandfather teaching his grandson about life. He told his grandson, "I feel as if I have two wolves fighting in my heart. One wolf is vengeful, angry, and violent. The other wolf is loving and compassionate." The grandson asked, "Which wolf will win the fight in your heart?" The grandfather answered, "The one I feed." That's why I seek God daily for His guidance, His power, His presence, and His abiding love. I will never be perfect, but I've asked God to "direct my steps" as He promises to do. What wonderful words when we get to heaven, and God lays a hand on our shoulder and says, "Well done, My good and faithful servant."

How I would treasure those words. I won't please everyone, but if I strive to please Him, that is really all that matters. Everything else will fall into place. "Seek the Kingdom of God above all else, and live righteously, and He will give you everything you need." (Matthew 6:33 NLT). I will be a better husband, dad, grandfather, brother, friend, and business man if I keep that perspective.

Well, here we are, not at the end of The Ride, but the beginning. There are adventures of faith awaiting me out there, and there may come a time when I will scarcely remember the man I use to be and the wasted years I spent in sin. In the meantime, He continues to shape me into the vessel He can use. Like the scripture, I am confident of this promise: "... that he who began a good work in you will carry it on to completion until the day of Christ Jesus," (Philippians

1:6 NIV). That is my prayer; "Finish what you started in me, Lord, in that cold, hard jail cell, looking down at my brother, feeling the shame of failing You above all."

Many opportunities are coming now to share my testimony with others, even those behind prison bars, who are desperate for hope and encouragement. Every time I stand to speak, I remember how God rescued and delivered me when everyone else had written me off as a bad seed, unsalvageable, used goods, definitely not ministry material. I smile at how God alone chooses whom He uses and feel blessed and honored to speak of His power and mercy any time, any place. "Just as He chose us in Him before the foundation of the world, that we should be holy and without blame before Him in love," (Ephesians 1:4 NKJV).

It pains me to think there may be a reader right now in a prison of your own making, and you don't see any way to break free. You may not be doing time in a real prison, but your life is locked up and held captive by bitterness, hate, alcohol, drugs, pornography, divorce, depression, anger, un-forgiveness, and self-loathing. What are you waiting for? Come to Jesus. He's like the loving father in the parable of "The Prodigal" who longs to open his arms to his wayward son. Run to Him, and let The Ride begin anew for you. He waits for you to come home. In the arms of the Savior, you will find true forgiveness and an amazing freedom you've never known.

By no means do I hope this happens soon, but there will come a day when they roll my casket down a church aisle, and Larry Andrews will be eulogized before loving friends and family. What will they say about me? They will dutifully read my birth and death date; often printed on the funeral program and grave stone with a dash in between. I am convinced it is what happens during that dash; your recorded life on earth, that really matters. A minister will say a few words regarding my life, but I hope someone will say, "He wasn't perfect. He lived two lives. One Before Christ; one after Christ claimed his life. He was full of joy and praise; he treasured his family and was a loyal friend. His life was an adventure few of us will ever understand. He was at his worst when he received God's best. He lived life to the fullest, and every day looked for opportunities to share Christ. His passion for God was contagious. Larry Andrews' life was not always easy, but he embraced every adventure of faith ... wow, what a ride!"

> *"This means that anyone who belongs to Christ has become a new person. The old life is gone; a new life has begun!" (2 Corinthians 5:17 NLT)*

~~~~~~~~

This is my prayer, taken from the book of Ephesians, for every person who will ever read this book:

> *"I pray that from His glorious, unlimited resources, He will empower you with inner strength through His Spirit.*
>
> *Then Christ will make His home in your hearts as you trust in Him. Your roots will grow down into God's love and keep you strong.*
>
> *And may you have the power to understand, as all God's people should, how wide, how long, how high, and how deep His love is.*
>
> *May you experience the love of Christ, though it is too great to understand fully. Then you will be made complete with all the fullness of life and power that comes from God." (Ephesians 3:16-19 NLT)*

FINAL THOUGHTS

Following is a principle God used to help me as I transitioned to my new life with Jesus Christ – I pray it speaks to your heart as well.

OWN IT!

Growing up with two brothers, there were plenty of occasions when none of us wanted to take the blame for the trouble we caused. I imagine Mom got pretty tired of hearing, "It's not my fault; he started it." More than once a day, one of us or all of us tried to sidestep any responsibility for the fight, the broken furniture, the lie that was told, or the mess we'd made. Dad was pretty quick to discipline *all* of us, because he couldn't pin-point exactly which kid was really to blame.

How refreshing it might have been if Mom were to hear just once, "Mom, it was me that hit him first. I started it, I deserve the punishment." She would have keeled over right there from the shock. My own children were no exceptions. There are always excuses for behaving badly, "Well, she made me so mad." Or, "It's his fault, he pushed me first." And on and on.

It doesn't change much after we reach adulthood. When we find ourselves in trouble, or in troublesome situations of our own making, we look for the excuses that got us there. It started with Adam who pointed the finger first. "Well, it was the woman You gave me, God, who made me eat the apple."

He was saying, "I am not to blame."

It is just human nature to try to wiggle free from any personal responsibility for our failures or shortcomings. We even try to list our excuses with God at times, but He knows the truth. Wouldn't it be easier just to come clean and own up to our mistakes, our poor choices, our sin?

1) One of the most important lessons I learned from my experience was to take ownership of the wrong I had done.

I broke the law. It wasn't the fault of my parents, law enforcement, the friends I hung with, or the temptations of the drug culture. IT WAS ME! And, I didn't go to prison for stealing a piece of bubble-gum. I was judged and sentenced because of my willing decision to do some pretty serious stuff.

Even while doing time, I met incarcerated men who could tick off on all their fingers the people that were to blame for the path that led them to prison. Sure, I realize that there are innocent people convicted for crimes they didn't commit, but most are serving time because they were proven guilty. Ultimately, there is only one person responsible for the life you live, and that is you.

Early in the legal process I saw no point in trying to side-step my lawless behavior. I knew the law, and I was fully aware when I was breaking it. In much the same way, it was also important when I received Christ as my Savior to acknowledge and admit my sins, so His grace could wash me clean. True repentance comes from a heart that yearns to be free, different, delivered. So, the first thing I learned along the ride - own it.

2) Own the fact that you are a sinner in need of a Savior. That pleases the Lord – He knows anyway. If we were perfect and our lives a never-ending fairytale of joy, what would be the point for salvation? What would we be saved from if we were perfect? Own the fact that you are not perfect.

Apostle Paul owned it. "This saying is reliable and deserves full acceptance: "Christ Jesus came into the world to save sinners – and I'm the biggest sinner of all." (I Timothy 1:15 CEB). I relate also to his anguished words in Romans 7:24 (NKJV), "O wretched man that I am! Who will deliver me from this *body of death?*"

I recall hearing of an old custom, a punishment in ancient times for those who had committed murder. The dead person's body was latched or chained to the murderer, and he could not be free from it. Soon, the decaying elements of disease or infection from the dead body overtook the murderer's own body, and he would die also. Paul may have been alluding to such a despicable state. Imagine being chained to a polluted corpse and unable to break free. No matter what we do, we cannot make the old man, the sinful self, clean, no matter how hard we try. Only Christ can deliver us from this "body of death."

A most poignant part of the traditional sinner's prayer goes, "Lord, I confess that I am a sinner." Nothing can happen, no repentance, no forgiveness, no everlasting salvation takes place until we own that one fact.

We also need to be quick to own other shortcomings as we see them occur in our lives, "Lord, I confess that I lied, was unfaithful, stole, embarrassed Your name, manipulated that situation, failed my wife, disappointed my child, etc. etc." Own it quickly, so you can get about the business of making it right.

Author, Jack Canfield writes, "It is only by acknowledging that you have created everything that has happened in your life up to this point, that you can take charge of creating the future you want." Which brings about the third point.

3) Own up to your past so Christ can erase it and give you a future. When we truly grasp the overwhelming power of God's mercy through Christ, we will walk in freedom like we've never known. Once I owned up to my mistakes, my bad choices, and my sin, it was His mercy and love that moved me to the next step: repentance. Sure, I didn't want to go to hell, but once I understood that I was His beloved, and He longs to have fellowship with me and give me an abundant life, that is when I promised to commit my life to serving Him. "… do you despise the riches of His goodness, forbearance, and longsuffering, not knowing that the goodness of God leads you to repentance?" (Romans 2:4 NKJV). God also reassures us in Jeremiah 29:11 (NIV), ""For I know the plans I have for you," declares the Lord, "Plans to prosper you and not to harm you, plans to give you hope and a future.""

I explain it this way. I know I caused my parents grief, but even when I was far away from God and living a life outside His will, there were certain things I could not or would not do, simply because I knew doing those things would break their hearts even more. It was their love and goodness that led me to refrain. The cost was simply too high.

Likewise, it is the goodness and grace of God that leads us to repent and want to please Him, not that He is holding a knife to our throats and the possibility of hell looms large. No, it is His abiding, matchless, miraculous love for us that should lead us to repentance. What do you do with a love so great that it sent God's only Son to die in your place?

I think of the parable of the prodigal son. First, he owned his situation, and it was bad. I love how the Word says it. The son who once had everything had hit bottom and the situation was dire. He suddenly woke up, like out of some dark stupor. "When he finally came to his senses …," (Luke 15:17 NLT), he recognized where he was and what he had done. He said, "I will go home to my father and say, "Father, I have sinned against both heaven and you." (Luke 15:18 NLT). It was the goodness of a father who drew the son to repent and come home again. You have only to read the story once to make the analogy clear. The prodigal's words, once he returned home, are honest, heartfelt, and humble. He owned it. No matter what you have done or experienced, go to God, our Father; He waits with open arms to embrace and forgive you.

When Naaman, the prophet, confronted David about his sin with Bathsheba, listen closely to what David said in response, "I have sinned against *the Lord*." You see, your sin or sins were not just against the law, or your wife, or your business partner, or some stranger. You and me, like David, have sinned against the Lord.

When the prodigal son returned home, he said, "Father, I have sinned against heaven and in your sight, and I'm not worthy to be called your son." What he is saying is true. He didn't just sin against a father who loved him, he had broken the heart of his heavenly Father. True repentance cancels all debts, and a new chapter can be written; restoration can now take place.

Then, lastly, own the fact that God has forgiven you completely and has a purpose for your life. Once you repent, don't live in that old life, under the old guilt, the condemnation, the shame any longer. We all know people who just can't get over the mistake or the failure in their lives. They have never moved past it; they talk about it, mourn over it, and their whole lives have revolved around that one bad choice they made – it may have been fifty years ago. Listen, when God forgives, He also forgets.

Once you have repented and asked God for forgiveness, you'll be the only one bringing it up again. As for the Lord, it was forgotten and removed "as far as the east is from the west". The old man you were, along with his sins were "cast into a sea of forgetfulness," the Word says. Embrace that, walk in it, live in that new-man freedom. Own who you are *now* in Christ; a new creation in Christ Jesus.

Here's the lesson in a nutshell. I hope you remember these three steps wherever you are along your life's journey. **Admit it - Repent it - Forget it.**

Admit it. Admit what? Admit that you had a part in determining the direction of your life. Admit that you may have harbored resentment, anger, and bitterness for situations and circumstances you felt were beyond your control. Admit and confess to any sin or sins that kept you from serving and pleasing God.

Repent it. Be truly broken hearted over the sin that brought pain to your life, the lives of others; and most of all, that you broke God's heart. That is the attitude God is looking for. We don't just sin against our spouses, or the government, or those who love us, no, we have sinned against God. He is the only one who can and will grant us grace and pardon when we truly repent; a word that means to do an about-face. You've been going in one direction and now you repent; you turn, you go in another direction. When you truly repent, you will change. Like the old chorus goes, "I have decided to follow Jesus – no turning back, no turning back."

Forget it. Satan, the accuser, wants you to never forget how bad, how undeserving, how terrible your sin was. However, you are limiting God's power of regeneration if you allow the enemy to constantly hold you hostage over your past. Don't let Satan shame you into living in the past. I know you can never truly forget what God saved you from. But, that is the point; He saved you. You are not that person any longer. "Never be a prisoner of your past. It was just a lesson, not a life sentence." (author unknown). These are marvelous truths we must continually throw in the devil's face. Declare them with me now:

"I am a new creation in Christ," (II Corinthians 5:17 NKJV).
"I am a child of God," (I John 3:1 NKJV).
"I am a friend of God," (James 2:23 NKJV).
"I am more than a conqueror through Him who loved us," (Romans 8:37 NKJV).

Own it - admit it, repent it, then forget it! Now, go on; walk in the newness of life. And if the transformation was real, don't be afraid to tell others about it! Your story will inspire others who need to hear it.

Larry Andrews

1 - Playing my Dad's guitar at age 4

2 - School photo – First Grade

3 - Senior Photo, Class of 1980

4 - Home Sweet Home in Washington, OK

5 - Summer of 1983; 21 years old. Little did I
know that this would come to pass...

6 - I finally made it to the "big time"

7 - The DOC bus, known as the "Green Lizard"

8 - The inside of the "Green Lizard" bus

9 - Arrival at LARC with hair, 3/29/2001

10 - Free haircut, provided by LARC on 3/29/2001

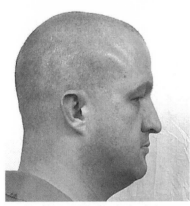

11 - My good side after the free haircut provided by LARC!

12 - Arrival at HMCC, 5/8/2002

13 - Taken at Davis Correctional Facility during my interview with reporter, Tom Lindley

14 - Performing in 2004 at the Prison Rodeo in McAlester, Oklahoma

15 - Me and Mom, Christmas 2007

16 - Mom and Dad, Christmas 2007

17 - Me and Dad, 2008 Idlett Family Reunion

18 - The final resting place for Mom and Dad in Washington, OK

19 - With my wife, Kim, attending the
Youth for Christ Banquet in 2018

20 - Speaking at God's Shining Light Church in
Tulsa, OK in 2019

21 - In the recording studio, working on my
upcoming EP release

22 - Taking a short break while out on a ride

23 - Visiting behind the fence at Joseph Harp
Correctional Center

24 - Reunion with former DOC Officer, and now
my friend, Vic "Stiemy" Williams

Photo Credits: 7, 8 - Oklahoma Department of Corrections, 13 - The Oklahoman, 21 - Michael Brown

The mission of Larry Andrews Ministries is to reach the lost with a message of hope.

To partner with Larry Andrews Ministries
Visit our website:
www.LarryAndrewsMinistries.com

For speaking inquiries, or to order
additional copies of **The Ride**
Visit our website:
www.LarryAndrews.com

Connect with Larry on Social Media
www.Facebook.com/AuthorLarryAndrews
Twitter and Instagram: @LarryAndrews777

45008712R00080

Made in the USA
Middletown, DE
13 May 2019